VGM Opportunities Series

OPPORTUNITIES IN
PHOTOGRAPHY
CAREERS

Bervin Johnson
Robert E. Mayer
Fred Schmidt

Revised by
Mark Rowh

Foreword by
Robert Heist, Jr.
Chairman
Department of Photographic Technology
Randolph Community College

VGM Career Horizons
NTC/Contemporary Publishing Group

TR
154
.J 64
1999

Library of Congress Cataloging-in-Publication Data

Johnson, Bervin M.
   Opportunities in photography careers / Bervin Johnson ; revised by
Mark Rowh. — Rev. ed.
      p.   cm. — (VGM opportunities series)
   Includes bibliographical references.
   ISBN 0-8442-6551-9 (hardcover). — ISBN 0-8442-6553-5 (pbk.)
   1. Photography—Vocational guidance.   I. Rowh, Mark.   II. Title.
III. Series.
TR154.J64   1998
770'.23—dc21   98-22684
                                                                        CIP

Cover photo credits:
Top left, courtesy Chimera Photographic Lighting; top right, courtesy Wolf
Camera, Inc., Atlanta, Georgia; bottom right, courtesy Sharon Hoogstraten;
bottom left, image copyright © 1998 Photodisc, Inc.

Published by VGM Career Horizons
A division of NTC/Contemporary Publishing Group, Inc.
4255 West Touhy Avenue, Lincolnwood (Chicago), Illinois 60646-1975 U.S.A.
Copyright © 1999 by NTC/Contemporary Publishing Group, Inc.
Printed in the United States of America
International Standard Book Number: 0-8442-6551-9 (cloth)
                                                     0-8442-6553-5 (paper)
18   17   16   15   14   13   12   11   10   9   8   7   6   5   4   3   2   1

DEDICATION

To our photographic mentors—the sharing, caring, knowledge-able individuals who help novice photographers become more proficient in the profession.

This book is dedicated to the late Clarence H. White, Jr., instructor, friend, and mentor. As an instructor at Ohio University in the 1950s, Clarence was an inspiration to all of his many photography students. He taught us to use photography creatively as a means of communication in a visually oriented world. His sage advice and guidance shaped students into true professionals, ready for any facet of photography they would pursue in later years.

CONTENTS

    History of photography. Modern photography. Future outlook.

    Approaches to training. Community and technical colleges. Trade schools. Degree programs. Canadian photo education programs. Workshop and short-term programs. Scholarships and financial aid.

    Experience in school. Strategies for obtaining employment. Attending conventions. Knocking on doors. Writing application letters. Using advertising to get employment. Advantages of a career in photography. Earning potential.

ABOUT THE AUTHORS

Bervin Johnson's work in the publication, commercial, industrial, portrait, freelance, and photography education fields has earned him national recognition as a photographer, exhibition judge, and educator, as well as the Qualified Professional Photographer rating from the Professional Photographers of America.

For seventeen years, he operated his own freelance photography business, doing assignments and furnishing stock photographs for many of the nation's largest advertising agencies and for industrial and publishing firms. His photographs and writings have been published throughout the United States and abroad while working for the *Oklahoma City Times & Oklahoman,* the *Dayton Journal-Herald, Sarasota Herald-Tribune, Birmingham News-Age-Herald, Atlanta Georgian,* and the Associated Press Southern Bureau. He is a charter-life member of the National Press Photographers Association (NPPA) and the Michigan chapter of the NPPA, and a life member of the Professional Photographers of America. He was a Michigan State University student advisor and supervised on-the-job training in photojournalism before he resigned to travel full-time for five years—to do a travelogue on *Magic Wonders of America.*

Bob Mayer's interest in photography started while attending high school in Columbus, Ohio, where he was active in the camera club. Evenings and for two summers he worked for a local photofinisher. During six years active duty in the U.S. Air Force, Mayer worked in base photo labs and in aerial photo reconnaissance labs. He then obtained both B.F.A. and M.F.A. degrees in photography from Ohio University. He worked in industrial photo studio management for several photographic manufacturers for more than seventeen years. During this time he lectured on photography all over the United States.

Mayer has taught photography at both Rochester Institute of Technology (RIT) and Arizona State University and for many years has been involved with teaching and coordinating short courses and workshops. He was a consultant on five volumes of the original *Life Library of Photography.* Currently a freelance writer/photographer, he is a contributing editor for *Shutterbug* and *Photomethods* magazines, where he has authored numerous feature articles on various photographic subjects and helps write monthly question-and-answer columns. He writes regularly for other publications, including *Law and Order* and *Photo Lab Management.* His professional guidebook on the Minolta Maxxum "i" series of cameras was published in 1991 by Hove Foto Books.

Fred Schmidt spent the first eighteen years of his life in Lone Wolf, Oklahoma, and environs. After service in the U.S. Coast Guard in World War II, he became interested in photography. He attended the Chicago School of Photography and began his career as an assistant photographer in a commercial studio there. Schmidt worked on several early television commercials and later wrote a column on color photography for *The National Photographer* magazine. He joined the Professional Photographers of America in 1955 and served as editor of *The Professional Photographer* for several years. In 1974 he was appointed editor of *Photomethods* magazine, a position he held for well over ten years.

Schmidt has been a guest lecturer in many high school and college photography classes; he was a curriculum advisor in photography for the Milwaukee Area Technical College. He also has organized and taught photography and electronic imaging courses.

FOREWORD

PHOTOGRAPHY: A PICTURE-PERFECT CAREER

Is it true that a picture is worth a thousand words? Millions of people must think so, because photography plays a tremendously important part in our everyday lives. Anyone can use a simple camera, and most people do. This means that amateur photography is big business, creating jobs for thousands of photographic technicians and others who work in manufacturing, sales, and processing industries.

At the other end of the spectrum from hobbyists and proud parents taking snapshots are professional photographers who pursue a variety of creative and challenging careers. Pick up a newspaper or magazine and you will see photos. Read a book, look at a CD cover, open a school yearbook, drive by a billboard advertisement... photographs are used everywhere. These professional photographers, using more complex equipment and taking advantage of greater knowledge than amateurs, fulfill a wide range of jobs that are often hidden from the general public. Most people are aware of the portrait photographers who make images of us at various times in our lives; but many people don't think of the photojournalists and the biomedical, industrial, scientific, and commercial photographers who advertise or illustrate what goes on in our society.

Almost no one thinks about the individuals who designed or manufactured the films we use or who are responsible for the processing and printing when the film has been shot. These photofinishing careers demand individuals with highly specialized skills and the creativity necessary to solve complex problems that face the photographic industry. In the past few years, there has been a major shift toward computer imaging that places new demands upon those involved in this side of the business.

Working as a photographer or as a photofinisher requires special training and abilities. If you are interested in the possibility of following a career related to these exciting professions, this book should prove quite helpful. It provides key information you will need to pursue such a career. The authors have outlined details you will need about the types of jobs available, job expectations, background and education needed, and other factors involved in a career. You're encouraged to use this book as an introduction to the job possibilities in this creative and challenging area. Perhaps your future holds a career behind the camera or in an equally important support role.

Robert Heist, Jr., Chairman
Department of Photographic Technology
Randolph Community College
Asheboro, North Carolina

ACKNOWLEDGMENTS

No book covering as wide a range of materials as this one could have been completed without the help of friends, colleagues, and experts in every area imaginable. To all of them, our gratitude is deep and warm. This career volume is truly a cooperative effort.

Special thanks to Douglas Stewart for the section on teaching. Thanks also to the following for reviewing and suggesting updates: Les Stroebel for sections of "Scientific and Technical Photography," Nile Root for "Biomedical Photography," Will Counts for "Photojournalism," Don Beyer for "Industrial Photography," Jerry Cornelius for "Commercial Photography," and Terry Klondaris for "Portrait Photography."

Thanks also to the following:

American Society of Media Photographers
Brooks Institute of Photography
Cathy Hefferin
Dakota County Technical College
Evidence Photographers International Council
Ithaca College
National Press Photographers Association
Photomarketing Association International
Randolph Community College
Rocky Mountain School of Photography
U.S. Department of Labor

INTRODUCTION

Photography is both an art and a craft. It offers a wide variety of career challenges to the person behind the camera as well as to the technician. Technological advances and new equipment continue to stimulate the increasing use of visual images for business, industry, and education. Many applications are also found in research, science, and engineering. A career in still photography can be one of the most satisfying experiences a person can have. It is, truly, a unique combination of art, craft, and business management.

Are you interested in photography for the money? Then forget it. There are many professions and crafts that pay a great deal more and require less work.

Are you interested in photography for the glamour? If so, forget it. Although the general public believes otherwise, few photographers get to photograph beautiful people or travel to exotic places in the line of duty.

But, if you want to go into photography with the idea of satisfying a need, or helping people to communicate better, or because of the challenges being a photographer offers—then you'll have little trouble making a success of your efforts.

The information that follows will help answer your questions about photography and assist you in choosing a career. The authors know only too well that the career decision you make now isn't necessarily forever. If this book contributes to your understanding of career opportunities in photography—or even if it influences you *not* to pursue photography as a career—we will have accomplished our goal.

CHAPTER 1

IMPORTANCE OF PHOTOGRAPHY

In the modern world, probably no other medium has more impact on everyday life than photography. We are influenced by visuals of all types, everywhere. Television, newspapers, magazines, computers, and books all use photography extensively to tell a story or capture our attention. Photography in commercials or print advertisements helps convince us we need a product or service.

No subject is too distant or too minute to photograph. Distant stars and planets, as well as the ocean floor and the world of microbes, are all explored and recorded with cameras of various designs and sizes. Images invisible to the eye are recorded clearly with the aid of infrared and ultraviolet films. Metals of all types are x-rayed in detail for observation and future use. Human bodies have been x-rayed for many years; today the computerized x-ray scanner, through transverse axial tomography, produces color x-ray cross-section profiles of the human body.

Millions of people throughout the world cannot read, and few people can read and comprehend more than 250 words per minute. As a result, photography has taken a leading role in communications. Regardless of the source of the original image (real life, art, dramatic staging), it is almost inevitable that eventually it passes through some means of photographic process. With the aid of machinery and electronics, the visual image has a decided edge over the written word. Too, the mind is capable of assimilating visual input faster than it can through the spoken or written word.

America's space program has been using photography from its beginning to record events and fascinate the world's population with images made from outer space. The quality of detail and speed of electronic transmission back to earth are indications that the future of photography is virtually limitless. In recent years, we have all been captivated by the images of distant planets made by unmanned space probes on their journeys through the solar system. The resulting pictures have expanded our knowledge of the universe.

The public is visually motivated in everything it does and sees. Television, movies, computer images, and printed photographs in our magazines and textbooks leave a lasting visual impression on everyone. Today's young people have grown up with and are being educated more and more with visual images.

The United States leads the world in picture taking, with about three-fourths of the nation's families owning at least one camera. Packing a camera and film is almost the first step in preparing for a vacation trip. Americans are such avid picture-makers that more than two million rolls of film are exposed each day (97 percent of which are color), and approximately 180,000 pictures are taken every hour.

Our high standard of living reflects the effectiveness of photography as it is used to appeal to our desires. Unconsciously we are sold cars, homes, food, fashions, and vacation trips to beautiful lands through photographic illustrations used in magazines, newspapers, television, billboards, and movies.

Not only is photography a hobby to millions of people, but it is also a major source of entertainment. Millions of people spend countless hours enjoying motion-picture films and televised movies in their homes and in theaters. Pictures are used to teach people how to do things and to convey information and ideas. Educational institutions, business, and industry are using more and more photographs, slides, videotapes, and motion pictures to train employees and salespeople in new skills of marketing and servicing of products.

The part photography plays in mass communication is increasing every day because it provides a method of duplication where one or ten million copies of any given photograph, drawing, or chart may be made quickly and easily for mass distribution. In fact, photography has been made so easy that a five-year-old child can be shown in just a few minutes how to take pictures with some of the fully automatic cameras on the market today.

With remote camera-satellites whirling millions of miles out in space, who knows what the future will bring in such a popular and diversified field as photography?

HISTORY OF PHOTOGRAPHY

The word *photography* derives from Greek words meaning "light" and "writing." The first experimental attempts at real photography were not undertaken until 1802, at which time Thomas Wedgwood, an English scientist, made photographic copies of paintings and worked with Sir Humphrey Davy in the production of silhouettes. Both Wedgwood and Davy made unsuccessful attempts to produce photographs of objects by means of a simple camera. Their early experiments were hampered by not knowing how to make pictures permanent.

In 1827 the French inventor Joseph Nicéphore Niépce made the first photograph, or *heliograph* ("sun writing"). He left his *camera obscura*—a large box with a tiny opening in one side that admitted light—sitting for eight hours, while it collected rays of light and projected them onto a pewter plate coated with bitumen of Judea, a light-sensitive chemical. He washed the plate in lavender oil and petroleum. On the plate remained an image of the roof and walls of his barn in the village of Saint-Loup-de-Varennes.

Daguerreotypes and Glass Plates

Daguerreotypes were developed in 1829 when Niépce joined with fellow French inventor Louis Daguerre to develop this remarkable achievement in photography. The big drawback to this new process was that no copies could be made from the plates. The first multiple printing came about in 1840, when the British inventor William Henry Fox Talbot introduced the *calotype* process, which produced a negative from light-sensitive paper.

The concern of improving negative quality led to the discovery of photographic glass plates in 1847 by Claude Felix Niépcé de Saint Victor. To make a photograph, the glass plate was coated with a mixture of silver salts and wet emulsion. The plate had to remain moist during exposure and developing, requiring that photographs be processed immediately after being taken.

Samuel F. B. Morse, inventor of the telegraph, contributed much to the progress of photography through his experimentations with daguerreotypes after the details of the process arrived in America in 1839. In fact, many gave him credit as being the father of American photography. He became one of the first instructors of photography, and among his many students was Matthew B. Brady, without a doubt the most famous American photographer of the nineteenth century. Brady developed a lucrative photography business with studios in New York and Philadelphia, which he later abandoned in order to photograph the Civil War. At the end of the war, Brady had a collection of 7,000 glass plates, including 30 he had made of Abraham Lincoln. He and his crew made these between the years 1860 and 1864. At that time, there were no extensive markets for his war pictures because newspapers and magazines had no way of reproducing them except by expensive engravings made by artists copying his photographs.

After the American Civil War, camera reporters began to show an interest in covering the growth of the frontier from the Mississippi River to the Rocky Mountains. Probably the most famous photographer of this movement was William Henry Jackson, who loaded a camera big enough to use 20" × 24" glass plates on a mule's back and joined the Hayden survey in 1875. Other mules were loaded with more cameras, lenses, glass plates, chemicals, trays, dark tents, and water for exploring the region now known as Yellowstone National Park. Jackson's scenic photographs of this area were used as the principal evidence in persuading Congress to establish the nation's first national park.

During the time that Jackson was photographing the wonders of Yellowstone, the British physician R. L. Maddox developed a light-sensitive gelatin emulsion that could dry on a plate without damaging the silver salts. Dry plates did not require immediate processing and thus offered freedom from the burden of the traveling darkroom.

Newspaper Photographs

The first newspaper halftone appeared in 1880 in the *New York Daily Graphic.* Along with the improvement of printing processes, the stature of the photographer also improved because of the distribution of photographs to thousands of viewers. With this sudden public exposure came a greater demand for photographs of all types. Studios became more numerous, and tremendous technical developments were made in all fields of photography. Because of the increasing demand for this new form of communication in a society of increasing complexity, the photographic industry emerged and blossomed, branching into specialized fields like portraiture, commercial photography, publication photography, photofinishing, and the manufacturing and sales of photographic supplies.

Photography for the Public

Any discussion of photography should include mention of George Eastman, the first manufacturer in the United States to formulate and put into practice large-scale camera production at low costs for the world market. It can truthfully be said that progress in photography goes hand in hand with the history and growth of the Eastman Kodak Company.

George Eastman, an American dry-plate manufacturer, advertised in 1884 that "shortly will be introduced a new sensitive film which is believed will prove an economical and convenient substitute for glass dry plates both for outdoor and studio work." This flexible, transparent film, plus an apparatus built simultaneously by American inventor Thomas Edison, made motion pictures successful.

In 1888, Eastman introduced the first Kodak camera. It was a box-type camera, lightweight and small, loaded with a stripping paper long enough for 100 exposures. The price of the camera loaded with film was $25. The camera and exposed film had to be shipped to Rochester, New York, in order to have the film removed and processed into prints and another strip of film loaded into the camera. The cost for this service was $10. The Kodak camera created an entirely new market and brought forth the phrase, "You press the button and we do the rest." Thus photography was simplified to the point where anyone could take pictures with a handheld camera simply by pressing a button.

Kodak's efforts have brought forth notable contributions to photography in the medical, scientific, educational, and entertainment fields. The introduction of Kodachrome color transparency film in 1935 revitalized the world of photography. Further improvements in films contributed much to the progress of the television industry, the data processing field, and space projects. Since 1935, a continuous evolution of improved products has been produced by sensitized goods manufacturers in the United States, Europe, and Japan. Users of both still and motion picture film and equipment continue to benefit from these product improvements.

One of the most significant developments in photography was the instant photography process, invented in 1947 by Dr. Edwin Land of the Polaroid Corporation. A new industry within photography was established, providing the image-maker with an invaluable tool and providing new employment opportunities.

MODERN PHOTOGRAPHY

Rapid developments in lighting, lenses, films, cameras, developers, and selling techniques advanced the photographer and the photographic profession to the level it enjoys today. Direct color photography now is used in all media and is in constant demand by the buying public. Other chapters of this book will go into more detail concerning the many types of photography and classifications of photographers.

One only needs to think of the high-quality, close-up photographs made of Mars and Saturn and other planets—high-speed motion picture cameras and the increasing number of photos appearing on the Internet—to get a picture of the pace photography is making in mass communications and the growing visual consciousness among people.

Advances in color emulsion technology have produced many brands of color slide and color negative films with normal ISO speeds of 1,600 ASA or more. A mere thirty years ago, even the fastest black-and-white films were only 400 ASA. These new films have broadened the appeal of amateur cameras that can produce an acceptable picture anywhere under any type of lighting.

Electronic Imaging

The most recent evolutionary step has been the development of electronic imaging. In the 1980s and 1990s, the use of video images in home situations via VCRs became accepted practice. More recently, digital cameras producing still photographic prints have become available.

Electronic still cameras were shown in prototype in the early 1980s. A Japanese newspaper photographer covering the 1984 Los Angeles Olympics was able to transmit electronic black-and-white pictures back to his newspaper in Tokyo within thirty minutes after taking them. Electronic scanner systems were then developed that permitted transmission of already processed 35mm color transparencies in about one minute. Both photographic and electronic images can be fed into electronic digital image processing units that can remove grain, improve sharpness, and alter color rendition. When images are digitized, a computer is used, via a keyboard, to retouch the image and alter its scale for page make-up prior to printing catalog or magazine pages.

Electronics are an increasingly integral part of photography as we know it today: in cameras, accessories, and processing laboratories. New developments in the technology of cameras, scanners, computers, and other types of equipment continue to change the ways photographs and other types of information are produced, distributed, and used. New job opportunities, and job descriptions, are being developed. Anyone entering the field of photography today will find it ever-changing and improving in the future.

FUTURE OUTLOOK

During the 1980s, the growth areas of the photographic industry overall were in increased sales of 35mm lens/shutter compact cameras, which accounted for about half of all cameras sold in the United States during 1989; the expansion of photofinishing, especially in the growth of one-hour minilabs; and the domination of the film market by color negative films, according to the *Wolfman*

Report. Single-use, disposable cameras also have grown in popularity since their introduction in 1987. During the 1990s the emphasis has been on the increased computerization of photography.

Electronic still photography equipment has been exhibited frequently at major conventions, and most major camera firms have introduced still video cameras, many of which are presently available for purchase. This type of photography is becoming increasingly common.

Harold Martin, editor of the *Wolfman Report,* summarizes that "photography has survived, continues to grow, and provides unequaled pleasure to billions of people around the world. 'Photography, the Universal Language' is no idle slogan. Present predictions of gloom based on electronic technology will both confirm the trend for expecting the worst and confound the prophets as the market will grow. Imaging technology may change, but the basic appeal of pictures will remain. And in years to come, imaging technology will play an important role in many aspects of life—education, communication, research, and leisure activities. The potential for growth remains impressive."

Employment of Photographers

According to the U.S. Department of Labor, about 139,000 people are employed as photographers in the United States. Some of the areas in which they hold jobs include the following:

commercial photography
media photography
portrait photography
scientific photography
photojournalism
television production
movie production
artistic photography

About four out of ten photographers are self-employed, which is a higher proportion than the average for all occupational areas. Many of those who are self-employed operate their own portrait studios or other small businesses specializing in photography. Some work on a freelance or contract basis for advertising agencies, magazines, website development specialists, portrait studios, police departments, or stock photo agencies.

Salaried photographers work in a variety of areas. Employers include the following:

photography studios
newspapers
magazines
advertising agencies
public relations firms
government agencies

Many jobs are salaried, and qualified individuals work a normal 35- to 40-hour week. The demand for commercial and portrait photographers remains relatively constant today. While some learn their skills by on-the-job training, more and more still photographers, especially those working for major firms as industrial photographers, must have advanced academic degrees in photography, or at least have graduated from one- or two-year practical-training courses.

Salaries

Salaries earned by photographers vary widely. Earnings differ by field of specialty, geographical area, experience, and other factors.

According to the National Press Photographers Association (NPPA), beginning salaries in the newspaper field range from $250 to $300 per week, or $13,000 to $15,600 annually. Experienced newspaper photographers may earn more than twice that amount.

According to the NPPA, pay in the television field averages about $500 per week after five years of experience, or $26,000 yearly. Photographers at larger newspapers and television stations tend to earn higher salaries than those serving smaller markets.

The U.S. Department of Labor reports that the average yearly salary for photographers and camera operators falls between $25,000 and $30,000. Some earn less than $15,000 a year, while others earn $50,000 or more.

Because circumstances vary so widely (one photographer might operate a lucrative studio in Beverly Hills, while another works for a small-town newspaper in rural Montana), "average" salaries have limited meaning when it comes to working in this field. Probably the best advice is to check with employers of photographers (or with practicing photographers) in your area and ask what income ranges are common. That way you'll get a feel for salaries that might be expected. Scanning the want ads can sometimes provide similar information.

Photo Lab Technicians

Photo lab technician skills still are often learned through on-the-job training, but there are a number of vocational training courses available for this specialty. This type of work is classified as not physically strenuous, but it tends to be very repetitive work done at a rapid pace, and workers are subject to eye fatigue. Work is generally in clean, well-lit areas (especially in the growing number of daylight-operated minilabs), but some of it is conducted in dimly lit darkrooms. Photo lab work usually involves a 40-hour week.

There are about 60,000 individuals who work as photo lab technicians, with about half of them working for large photofinishing labs. They earn an average salary of about $350 per week, according to the U.S. Department of Labor, although salaries vary and some earn upwards of $600 weekly.

Canadian Outlook

We spoke with several professional photographers in Canada who commented that there are lots of opportunities for photographers there, especially around major population centers. They said there is always a demand for qualified photo lab technicians.

One Canadian photo writer said there are always opportunities for skilled and experienced photographers who know what they are doing. Since the population is smaller than that of the United States, and there are fewer firms using photography, competition is tougher. Canadian photographers have to generalize more to serve a broader client base and not try to be specialists in just one type of photography.

The Professional Photographers of Canada (PPofC), P.O. Box 337, Gatineau, Quebec, Canada J2F 6JE, is an active group of professionals that was formed in 1946 by a group of commercial and press photographers. They share their photographic expertise through a bilingual publication, published six times a year, and an annual convention. There are seven provincial chapters throughout Canada. You should be able to obtain current and pertinent advice from local members of this group to assist you in finding schooling or employment in the field of photography in Canada.

CHAPTER 2

LEARNING THE CRAFT

Like any other craft that includes creative skill as well as knowledge, photography has no hard and fast rules for success. However, some clues can be obtained from observing the traits of contemporary photographers in their manner of work and living.

Patience, persistence, an inquisitive mind, enthusiasm, a desire to learn, creativity, and a genuine interest in nearly everything are the major personal qualifications for getting started in photography. Good people skills are also important. Seriousness of purpose and a willingness to assume greater responsibilities are clues that do not go unnoticed when advancement opportunities arise.

If you are interested in a basic 40-hour workweek, doing some detailed operation for an established photographic business or industrial photography department, you do not need to have a great amount of ambition. But you should have a goal or dream to be the best photographer in your school, in your community, in your state, or in your professional associations in order to get to the top in your field. When you feel this way about your work, you will find it fun and enjoyable—in fact, your livelihood then ceases to feel like work.

Dependability is another key to success. In the photographic profession, many appointments and deadlines must be met and completed on time. Willingness to give service is most important in choosing photography as a profession. Working long hours, late

13

at night, weekends, and some Sundays and holidays is often necessary to become successful in many fields of photography. Attendance at conventions and seminars, as well as taking advantage of refresher courses, is important in order to keep up with the constant progress in the photographic world.

You will progress faster in most areas of photography by being artistically inclined or having some art background. To go to the top, a photographer needs to know the basics of photography and something about bookkeeping, purchasing, electronics, optics, graphic reproduction, color, architecture, anatomy, lighting, advertising, public relations, and psychology, as well as knowledge of what is going on in the community, the nation, and the world.

In no other profession or trade could you find such a diversified and interesting challenge. If you want to know about all these things and are enthusiastic about doing them, you should go far. Your chances of finding success and enjoyment in photography are greater if you possess these attributes.

Professional organizations are placing increased emphasis upon educational programs. Manufacturers and distributors are making contributions and working with educational institutions in developing new courses in photography. Upgrading curricula, textbooks, equipment, and faculties is recognized as a top priority project by all.

APPROACHES TO TRAINING

Any student contemplating enrolling in any advanced course in photography should be aware that there are two general approaches. Professionally oriented programs are structured to prepare the student to produce still or motion pictures according to the requirements specified by their clients or employers. Other courses have a fine arts basis of instruction. These courses help the individuals sharpen their artistic and creative visions rather than teach them how to produce images to meet commercial needs.

Both types of courses tend to provide students with an academic background in the fundamentals of photography, its history, and current processes and various methods necessary to produce photographic images. The obvious differences are in the final use of the photograph produced, or who pays for the print.

In general, community colleges and trade schools tend to offer more technical courses where most of the work is related to the major subject area of photography. Conversely, students who attend four-year colleges or universities only have one-fourth to one-third of their courses in their major (photography) area. The bulk of the additional credit courses are in other subjects, such as the humanities, sciences, mathematics, communications, and various electives. A graduate from a four-year program generally has a broader, more diversified background, but it takes two additional years and more tuition to achieve this diversification, and the individual will enter the job market later to begin earning a living.

There are many specializations within the separate fields of motion pictures and video, still photography, and graphic arts. Most students entering a vocational field seldom are aware of the variety of jobs and specializations available to graduates. A listing of the various positions filled by recent graduates of photographic programs may be helpful. Since any one of these areas of specialization may not be in great demand several years in the future, it would be wise to take courses that overlap whenever possible.

A few of the more than a thousand schools offering courses in photography are listed in Appendix C. An important decision for you to make—no matter if you are still in high school or have completed school and are contemplating changing to the photography profession—is whether you can afford the time and cost of getting as much academic education as possible before pursuing a lifetime career. If you decide you can afford it, this list of schools for photographic training will be worth your writing to get additional information concerning their courses and costs.

Due to the rapid pace at which photography is moving today as a communications medium, combined with the spiraling cost of everything in general, any list of costs of courses offered by various schools would be inaccurate by the time this book is printed. In general, if you are fortunate enough to be able to travel to the location of your preferred school and choose your course of study, you will have a wide selection of offerings: a one-day "Flying Short Course" given each year in selected localities by the National Press Photographers Association; two-day to one-week refresher courses offered through the entire year at the Winona International School of Professional Photography in Mt. Prospect, IL; evening courses offered by adult education programs in your community or nearest city; and curricula leading to the highest academic degrees.

Some high schools offer courses in photography, and a relative few have full-fledged programs. For example, Lincoln High School in San Jose offers an advanced multimedia program that includes an emphasis on digital photography. But in most cases, you will need to study at a trade or technical school, community college, or university to earn a degree or diploma in photography.

Because many photographic curricula are adapted to accept whatever the particular department has in the way of related subjects and instructors, there is no model or standard curriculum for photography education. To help prospective students of photography and counselors in advising them on curricula being offered in some schools, the authors, in the following pages, will refer specifically to those used in the Dakota County Technical College; Milwaukee Area Technical College; Hallmark Institute of Photography; Rochester Institute of Technology's School of Photographic Arts and Sciences; and Brooks Institute of Photography.

COMMUNITY AND TECHNICAL COLLEGES

The American Association of Community Colleges, One Du-Pont Circle, Washington, DC 20036, is the best source of up-to-date information at the two-year college level.

Directories, available in some school and public libraries, containing names and addresses of many community and junior colleges with requirements for admission to each college, enrollment, descriptions of the campus facilities, curricula offered, costs, and financial aid available, are:

American Association of Community Colleges Annual Directory
One DuPont Circle
Washington, DC 20036

Peterson's Guide to Two-Year Colleges
P.O. Box 2123
Princeton, NJ 08543

There is a wide variety in photography curricula, some quite good and others not as well-planned, offered on the junior college or community college level. Many of them are quite basic.

Dakota County Technical College

A good example of a comprehensive photography program at the community college level is the program offered by Dakota County Technical College in Rosemount, Minnesota. This college offers six different programs related to photography. These range in length from a two-year, associate degree program requiring the completion of 96 quarter-hour credits, to a short (16-credit) certificate program. Following is an overview of the requirements of each program.

A.A.S. Degree, Photographic Technology (pending state approval): 55 credits in photography and related courses, plus electives and general education requirements totaling 96 credits.

Diploma, Photographic Technology: 46 credits in photography and related courses and 2 elective credits.

Certificate, Mini Lab Operator: 12 credits consisting of four courses related to photo processing, plus technical electives totaling 4 credits.

Certificate, Photographer Assistant: 17 credits in photography courses.

Certificate, Professional Lab Technician: 29 credits in courses related to photography and lab work, plus 3 elective credits.

Certificate, Electronic Imaging Technician: 36 credits in courses related to photography, printing, and electronic imaging.

Milwaukee Area Technical College

The Milwaukee Area Technical College (MATC) also has an impressive photography program. Program offerings at MATC include the following:

TECHNICAL COURSES

View Camera Techniques
Photographic Trends
Photographic Lighting
Measurement Techniques
Color Photography 1
Commercial Photography
Portraiture
Color Photography 2
Photographic Portfolio
Photojournalism
Industrial Photography
Photographic Internship

TECHNICAL SUPPORT COURSES AND ELECTIVES

Design and Composition
Fundamental Photography

Photographic Machine and Process Monitoring
Digital Darkroom Techniques
Drawing Techniques
Survey of Digital Photography
Digital Photography
Advanced Studio Lighting
Candid and Formal Wedding Photography
Introduction to Printing
Introduction to Computers

Typical Courses Offered in Community and Technical College Photography Programs

Beginning Camera Techniques
Black/White Processing and Printing
Custom Black/White Printing Techniques
Photographic Chemistry
Photographic Science
Process Monitoring for Color
Professional Portrait Photography
Introduction to Professional Printing
Professional Color Printing
Machine Printing and Proofing
MiniLab Systems
Copy and Restoration
Commercial Photography
Introduction to Electronic Imaging
Introduction to Photoshop
Introduction to Graphic Communication
Line Photography Theory
Line Photography Lab
Stripping I
Halftone Photography
Customer Relations in Trade and Technical Industries
Lab Technician and Management

Photography Workshop I
Photography Workshop II
Special Projects Workshop III
Advanced Process Monitoring
Advanced/Specialized Photography
Color Print Enhancement Techniques
Introduction to Photo Technology
Photographic Internship
Basic Object Lighting
Introduction to Digital Imaging
Photojournalism

TRADE SCHOOLS

Technical and trade schools have more specialized curricula. They are streamlined and free of the usual academic studies normally a part of photography courses in colleges and universities. In these schools, you learn by doing and work under the immediate supervision of an instructor.

Trade schools seem to be growing in popularity, since there are increasing numbers of them across the country. The mere fact that students receive more intensive training, and therefore complete their training in one or two years, is appealing to many individuals with a desire to learn photography but with a limited budget for schooling.

To obtain a better idea of the types of vocational training currently available, look in your local library for the *Directory of Public Vocational Technical Schools and Institutes,* published by Media Marketing Group & Minnesota Scholarship Press, Inc., P.O. Box 611, DeKalb, IL 60115. This book lists schools and institutes in alphabetical order by name of each school within each state.

Pertinent categories listed under photography schools and courses include:

Photo Equipment Technician
Photographic Technician
Photography
Photography and Film Communications
Photography Commercial/Professional
Photo Lab Technician
Photojournalism

Hallmark Institute of Photography

The Hallmark Institute of Photography in Turner Falls, Massachusetts, is one school that provides specialized photographic training in only ten months. Hallmark takes pride in its atmosphere of real-world experience in photography, which is structured more as a photographer/client relationship rather than as student/teacher.

Hallmark offers an intensive schedule requiring student attendance and involvement on a Monday-through-Friday, full-day basis, with occasional evening and weekend assignments. To complete this accelerated program, a cumulative total of approximately 1,400 class hours in 40 weeks is required, which is said to be the equivalent of nearly two years of traditional academic schedules. Although about 65 percent of this class time is related to photography, the remainder is devoted to such related academic and business subjects as finance, marketing, business management, and personnel, subjects that are essential to surviving as a photographer today.

Although not all Hallmark graduates decide to actually pursue a career in photography immediately after graduation, better than 80 percent of the graduates find successful employment, the majority working for small studios or becoming self-employed. The faculty and staff are experienced working professionals who teach subjects with which they deal on a day-to-day basis.

Photofinishing Schools

Probably the most successful of all photography education programs, from the standpoint of consistently placing graduates into meaningful, well-paying positions, is photofinishing. All of the schools with two- or four-year courses in this technical specialization now have one or more operating minilabs for students to work with while learning, in addition to the large-volume photofinishing equipment customarily found in big, high-volume labs. Therefore, students can become familiar with operating and repairing the equipment found in the majority of processing labs. Most photofinishing schools report nearly 100 percent placement of recent graduates.

Schools offering specialized training programs in photofinishing include:

- Dakota County Technical Institute, Rosemount, Minnesota
- Lansing Community College, Lansing, Michigan
- Randolph Community College, Asheboro, North Carolina
- Rochester Institute of Technology, Rochester, New York

Full mailing addresses of these schools are found in Chapter 9.

Major manufacturers of photographic processing equipment—such as Gretag, Hope, Fuji, Lucht, Kodak, and Kreonite—along with the leaders in minilab photofinishing equipment, contribute their expertise, equipment, and support to expand the educational facilities in photographic processing engineering technology to keep these courses current with state-of-the-art equipment.

DEGREE PROGRAMS

There are over 800 departments offering courses that lead to degrees in photography and related fields. Some schools have more than one department with photographic courses, so there are fewer than 800 schools with such courses. Some of these schools are listed in Appendix C.

An example of a comprehensive photography program at the bachelor's degree level is provided by Ithaca College in Ithaca, New York. Ithaca's Roy H. Park School of Communications offers majors in cinema, photography, film, and visual arts among other related programs. An especially attractive element at Ithaca is its program of internships. Recent students have earned professional experience at Eastman Kodak, CNN, and other leading organizations.

Another example is the bachelor's degree program with a major in photography offered by Northern Arizona University. This program combines three major areas of study to prepare students with both technical and management knowledge. These areas are:

technical and creative skills in photography
sound business basics
an introduction to the arts and sciences

At Northern Arizona, students complete ten photography classes plus communication classes, liberal arts requirements, electives, a minor, and an internship.

Two of the best known schools offering degree programs are the School of Photographic Arts and Sciences at the Rochester Institute of Technology and Brooks Institute of Photography.

Rochester Institute of Technology

The School of Photographic Arts and Sciences at the Rochester Institute of Technology (RIT) offers undergraduate two-year

(A.A.S.) and four-year (B.F.A., B.S.) degrees, and graduate-level (M.F.A., M.S.) degrees. All levels of degrees are offered in a variety of photographic specializations.

The primary goal of the RIT professional photography curriculum is to prepare the individual student for a career involving photography as a chief means of support.

Undergraduate courses are offered in seven subject areas:

Biomedical Photographic Communications
Film and Video
Imaging and Photographic Technology
Photographic Processing and Finishing Management
Advertising Photography
Photojournalism
Fine Arts Photography

The current RIT course catalog lists more than 180 courses in the School of Photographic Arts and Sciences. A brief sampling of course titles at this school includes:

Biomedical Photo I and II
Film History & Aesthetic
Portable Video Production
Visual & Commercial Film Production
Sound Recording
Photography Core
Photographic Workshop
Animation & Graphic Film
Applied Photo I and II
Creative Problems
Photojournalism I and II
Advertising Illustration
Portraiture
Photo Process Control
Color Transparency Processing Techniques
Materials and Processes of Photography

Color Printing Theory
Color Photo Design
Introduction to Dye Transfer
Holography I
High-Speed/Time-Lapse
History & Aesthetics of Photography
Photography as a Fine Art
Survey of Imaging Science
Geometric Optics
Optical Engineering

In addition, independent studies and group seminars are arranged throughout the year to explore specialized techniques in photography. Some short workshops and seminars are offered during summer months.

Brooks Institute of Photography

Another highly respected, independent photography school is Brooks Institute of Photography in Santa Barbara, California. Brooks offers a Bachelor of Arts degree in professional photography and a graduate-level program leading to the Master of Science degree. Photographic-major programs offered at Brooks include:

Color Technology
Commercial
Illustration/Advertising
Digital Imaging
Digital Media
Industrial/Scientific
Media
Motion Picture/Video
Portraiture

Among the photographic courses listed in the Brooks catalog are:

Conceptual Photographic Illustration
Video Production
Photography as an Analytical Tool
Photojournalism Techniques
Advanced Nature Photography
Undersea Photography Technology
Portraiture Fundamentals
Advanced Portrait Techniques
Advanced Multimedia Projects
Digital Imaging
Web Page Development

Typical Four-Year College/University Course Titles in Photography and Related Areas

Introduction to Photography
History of Photography
Contemporary Photographic Issues
Introduction to Black-and-White Photography
Color Photography
Photography: Advanced Studio
Documentary Photography
Photojournalism
Advertising and Illustration Photography
Film Production
Publications Photography
Studio Photography
Location Photography
Industrial Photography
Portfolio Development
Introduction to Layout and Design

CANADIAN PHOTO EDUCATION PROGRAMS

Most of the college-level photography courses offered in Canada are found in the Province of Ontario in two-year programs at junior colleges, which are called colleges of applied arts and technology. Some offer fields such as multimedia production and film production, which include courses related to photography. These colleges include:

Algonquin College of Applied Arts and Technology
140 Main Street
Ottawa K1S 1C2

Confederation College of Applied Arts and Technology
P.O. Box 398
Thunder Bay P7C 4W1

Fanshawe College of Applied Arts and Technology
1460 Oxford Street
London 95W 5H1

Humber College of Applied Arts and Technology (photo lab tech)
205 Humber College Boulevard
Toronto M9W 5L7

Loyalist College of Applied Arts and Technology (photojournalism)
P.O. Box 4200
Belleville K8N 5B9

Sheridan College of Applied Arts and Technology
1430 Trafalgar Road
Oakville L6H 2L1

A Bachelor of Applied Arts degree in commercial and industrial photography is offered by:

Ryerson Polytechnical Institute
350 Victoria Street
Toronto M5B 2K3

Several Canadian institutions in locations other than the Ontario area offer advanced photography instruction. These include:

Alberta College of Art and Design
   1407 Fourteenth Avenue NW
   Calgary, AL T2N 4R3

A bachelor's degree in photography is available through:

University of Victoria
   P.O. Box 1700
   Victoria, BC V8W 2Y2

WORKSHOP AND SHORT-TERM PROGRAMS

In addition to degree and certificate programs, there are a number of outstanding short workshop programs available on most every facet of photography. You will find these programs mentioned in greater detail in Chapter 10.

Some schools operate short-term programs that provide concentrated training in photography. For example, the Rocky Mountain School of Photography in Missoula, Montana, offers a "Summer Intensive Program" covering seventeen specific topics. Individual courses consist of 4 to 32 classroom hours of instruction, totaling 261 hours over an eleven-week period.

These summer courses include:

Basic Photographic Studies (20 hours)
Basic Black-and-White Darkroom (20 hours)
Field Class (25 hours)
History of Photography (8 hours)
Advanced Photographic Studies (20 hours)
Advanced Darkroom (16 hours)
Zone System of Exposure (8 hours)

Introduction to Medium Format (8 hours)
Introduction to Large Format (8 hours)
Photographic Lighting (32 hours)
Photography of People (16 hours)
Business and Marketing (16 hours)
Portfolio (20 hours)
Special Topics (Guest Instructors) (32 hours)
Stock Photography (4 hours)
Handcoloring (4 hours)
Introduction to Digital Imaging (4 hours)

SCHOLARSHIPS AND FINANCIAL AID

The rapid rise in college expenses over the last decade has far outstripped the rise in most other living costs, and the spiral at this time seems endless.

A student going to a public university, if he or she is a resident of the state, will typically spend a total of approximately $7,000 to $10,000 per year. In some cases, the outlay will run substantially higher. Basic yearly charges at private universities average $15,000 to $20,000 or more. Books, clothing, transportation, and other expenses can add another $2,000 to $3,000 to the basic costs. Since the cost of supporting educational institutions is going up yearly, it would be best to write to the colleges or universities you would be interested in attending to get the latest tuition rates and charges for room and board.

Tuition Assistance

Although costs have risen considerably, the College Scholarship Service reports that it is now easier for families of all income levels to qualify for government-subsidized student loans through the

Stafford Loan program. Most leading banks have further details on these low-interest educational loans. Several other loan and grant programs are available for those demonstrating financial need.

Economic trends have helped to increase the popularity of two-year community colleges, where students can live at home. They also have increased the pressure for more scholarships for students, as well as more government aid to colleges and universities.

Due to the surprising number of financial aid programs and scholarships, along with the increasing opportunities to obtain work while going to school, it is safe to say that serious students can manage some way to work and borrow themselves through almost any course of education they choose to pursue.

Most schools offering photography courses also have qualifications information for applicants on scholarships. These will gladly be explained for the asking.

The Photographic Society of America (PSA) annually awards stipends to provide tuition assistance in the amount of $1,500. Those stipends are available to photo career freshmen at both the Brooks Institute of Photography and the Rochester Institute of Technology. Full-time students at either school may apply through the school for these scholarships in the spring of their freshman year. Both a written application and a portfolio of the individual's work are requested.

Other Scholarships and Grants

Not all scholarships are tied into college tuition. Many states have a Council on the Arts or similarly named groups that offer annual monetary grants for individuals working in various artistic fields, including photography and filmmaking. Check references in your local library to determine the name, or names, of any groups in your state and write for information. You might qualify for a grant, scholarship, or research fellowship.

PHOTO CONTESTS

Numerous photographic contests are conducted by various organizations each year. Some offer quite respectable cash prizes or equipment. State fairs have contests for many different subjects, including photography. You will never know just how good your own photography is until you enter some prints to be judged by qualified experts.

INTERNSHIPS

Internship programs are offered to a few selected students by:

The International Center of Photography
    1130 Fifth Avenue
    New York, NY 10028

Internships for museum work are offered by:

The International Museum of Photography
    George Eastman House
    900 East Avenue
    Rochester, NY 14607

Several newspapers offer internships in photography. These are usually summer positions for students to fill in for vacationing staff photographers. Inquire about internships at newspapers in your area.

KODAK SCHOLARSHIPS

The Eastman Kodak Company has awarded endowed scholarships to several major photographic colleges and universities. In addition, Kodak has been awarding one-time scholarships for the value of actual in-state tuition for one academic year (up to a maximum of $2,000 each) to thirty institutions around the United States. These one-time scholarships are awarded to full-time students who have completed one full year of course work. Students of both two-year associate programs and four-year bachelor's degree programs are eligible.

REFERENCE MATERIALS

Your local library should have copies of reference books for all types of financial assistance, such as *The College Board Scholarship Handbook*. Listed therein are several scholarships, ranging from $100 to $4,000, for various areas of photography. Sources of financial assistance available to college students are described in these reference books:

Foundation Grants to Individuals
    The Foundation Center
    79 Fifth Avenue
    New York, NY 10103

Bear's Guide to Finding Money for College
    Ten Speed Press
    P.O. Box 7123
    Berkeley, CA 94707

The College Board Scholarship Handbook
    The College Board
    45 Columbus Avenue
    New York, NY 10023–6992

Don't Miss Out: The Ambitious Student's Guide to Financial Aid
    Octameron Associates
    1900 Mt. Vernon Avenue
    Alexandria, VA 22301

Free Money for College
    Facts on File
    11 Penn Plaza
    New York, NY 10011

CHAPTER 3

GETTING STARTED
IN PHOTOGRAPHY

Almost everyone learns to use a camera, but most people remain amateurs. Those who take their work to an increasingly higher level form the pool from which professional photographers are drawn.

So how do you know if you have the potential for professional photography? First will come a compelling desire to produce images that attract the attention of others. The intensity of your desire to improve will determine how many rolls of film you expose and whether you choose to do your own darkroom work or send your film to a photofinisher.

In getting started, consider visiting camera shops and attending amateur photography club meetings in your high school or community. This will broaden your knowledge of the fundamentals of picture making. If you have managed to invest in a camera of your own, with interchangeable lenses and a light meter (if there is none in the camera), you now are on your way to making better photographs. The next step would be to look for an enlarger, three or four small trays, and a room you can close off to have complete darkness—then you are in business. You also will need processing chemicals.

After you have made exposures in your camera (taken pictures), processed your films, and made some prints from your negatives, you should be eager to print larger and better pictures. This is the point at which you should be reading more photography magazines and books and arranging to visit some advanced amateur's setup or a professional photographer's studio. Observing the type and amount of equipment used by them will show you what you are getting into. Only by asking questions will you learn what expenses you will have if you decide to expand your own darkroom facilities and camera equipment.

After your visits to camera stores, an amateur's darkroom, or to a professional photographer's studio, as well as talking to your counselor in school—provided you are still a student—you should know how strong your desire is to advance in the photography field.

Let us assume you now own a good camera (35mm or 120 size), have read some books, have a darkroom setup of your own, have exposed some films and made prints, and have visited camera stores and a professional photography studio. The next step would be to think of finding part-time work helping a professional photographer in any capacity available.

EXPERIENCE IN SCHOOL

Most high schools have a darkroom with some equipment, a student newspaper, a camera club, or a yearbook. Let it be known that you would like to be a staff member of one of the student publications and join the camera club. Architects and school boards across the country have incorporated darkrooms and facilities in school buildings because photography has become so important to communication programs. Also, high school camera clubs have proven to be valuable to the schools in gaining additional publicity and recognition in local newspapers, besides providing greater pictorial coverage for yearbooks and student newspapers.

A fine organization with an impressive photography program, active in many rural high schools, is the 4-H Clubs of America. Information on this organization's photography program may be obtained by contacting your local high school principal, the office of your county Cooperative Extension Service, your state department of agriculture, or by writing directly to the 4-H Program Extension service.

If you are going to be active in your camera club, 4-H project, or the yearbook or student newspaper staff, don't overlook the chance of making some outside money to pay the costs of your equipment and materials. This can be done by making the acquaintance of your neighborhood newspaper editor to see if you can furnish occasional photographs of school activities for use in the newspaper. Selling extra prints from your negatives to students and their parents is another income-producing idea that will help you increase and improve your photographic equipment and knowledge.

When you start showing some monetary return on your photography investment, you will have a new and different outlook on photography as a valuable lifetime hobby or profession. This also could be the beginning of your career in the business world. Thousands of high school graduates have gone into trade schools and colleges with high school photography experience and earned their tuition, cost of books, and room and board by selling photographs on campus or working as a technician or photographer with student publications. In addition, remember that you could still represent your college, neighborhood, or weekly or daily newspaper as a campus photographer. Remember, too, that the hometown newspaper editor could use that occasional photograph of the community's students receiving recognition while away at college.

An example of being successful in working one's way through college by selling photographs is Victor Keppler. By taking pictures and selling them wherever he could, Mr. Keppler was able to work his way through high school, college, and law school. He did so well financially and enjoyed photography so much that he continued to become one of America's most successful professional photographers. The history of photography lists many other big names who worked their way to the top with photography while learning all they possibly could about the profession.

You would not need to wait until you have gone to college or received a degree in photography to start making a name for yourself. High school is a good time to start, even though many have started gaining recognition after graduating from college and even after retirement from other professions.

Even though photography as a hobby or as a profession can be rewarding from a monetary standpoint, we would not recommend going into the profession purely for the sake of making money. Be sure that photography is the one occupation that will give you the most pleasure and personal satisfaction. If there is another profession that comes to mind that would give you more enjoyment, then pursue it, and use photography as a hobby or sideline.

Competitions

In high school you should start making exhibition prints or slides for camera club exhibits and entering competitions such as the annual competition sponsored by the National Scholastic Press Association. This competition is excellent for rating your ability compared with other high school photographers throughout the country. If you are unable to get information on this contest through your school, write to:

National Scholastic Press Association
   2221 University Avenue SE
   Minneapolis, MN 55414

Other competitions are sponsored by 4-H Clubs of America and Boy and Girl Scouts of America.

Besides the cash and scholarships you get from photo contests, the recognition, publicity, and satisfaction of winning top awards for your creative ability is something that you could never place a monetary value on.

For information on photography opportunities in these organizations, write:

Boy Scouts of America
 1325 Walnut Hill Lane
 P.O. Box 152079
 Irving, TX 75015

Girl Scouts of the USA
 420 Fifth Avenue
 New York, NY 10018

National Council of the YMCAs of the USA
 101 North Wacker Drive
 Chicago, IL 60606

YWCA of the USA
 726 Broadway
 New York, NY 10003

Several major professional photographic organizations listed below offer reduced-rate student memberships to individuals studying photography on an advanced level. Joining one or more organizations that deal with a specialized area in which you are interested often provides you with mailings, publications, and the opportunity to attend the annual convention as a member. At the convention, you may make contacts that will help you further your career plans, or even find employment after graduation.

Photo Marketing Association International (PMAI) and its off-shoot groups—Professional School Photographers Association of America, Society of Photo Finishing Engineers, and Society of Photographic Counselors—all have this common address:

PMAI
   3000 Picture Place
   Jackson, MI 49201

Other organizations include the following:

Advertising Photographers of New York
   27 Twentieth Street
   New York, NY 10011

American Society of Media Photographers (ASMP)
   14 Washington Road, Suite 502
   Princeton Junction, NJ 08550-1033

Canadian Association of Photographers and Illustrators in
      Communications (CAPIC)
   100 Broadway Avenue, Suite 322
   Toronto, ON M4M 2E8
   Canada

International MiniLab Association (IMA)
   2627 Grimsley Street
   Greensboro, NC 27403

National Press Photographers Association, Inc. (NPPA)
   3200 Croasdaile Drive, Suite 306
   Durham, NC 27705

Professional Photographers of America (PPofA)
   57 Forsyth Street
   Atlanta, GA 30303

Professional Photographers of Ontario
   2833 Donelly Drive, RR #4
   Kemptville, ON K0G 1J0
   Canada

Photographing family pets, younger brothers and sisters, and the
neighbor's children is the way many professional photographers
got their start in making pictures for a living. After photographing
children and pets and selling prints to help with the purchasing of

more film and equipment, word passes on to relatives and friends, who in turn want more pictures made. As the volume of business increases, so do the facilities for processing, printing, and photographing. The next move usually is into making portraits and photographing weddings. This is probably why many photographers who got their start in this manner often end up owning portrait studios or working with other portrait photographers.

STRATEGIES FOR OBTAINING EMPLOYMENT

Once you have had the experience of working for a camera shop, professional photographer, or in a company photographic department, you have made the first step toward obtaining future employment. It is through these valuable contacts that you learn of other photographers and photographic establishments. Always take advantage of new contacts in the photographic world. Talk with all the photographers you can and ask questions about things you do not understand. Let it be known at your camera club and photographic meetings that you are interested in a job where you can get more photographic experience. In most cases, you stand a better chance of getting the kind of job you want if you know a specific person to contact, rather than simply placing an application through a personnel office. Sometimes, however, the latter is the only way you have to make a contact in distant locations and with large company photographic departments.

Unless you have been fortunate enough to have had the time and facilities in high school or college to make a good assortment of enlargements of diversified subject matter to show a prospective employer, you will have to rely on making a good impression in your interviews. Much will depend on your appearance, speech, eagerness to get the job, and references from former employers and school professors. Here, too, prizes, awards, and recognition gained through photography contests will be most helpful to you. If nothing else, having won awards shows an extra interest in photography. This will be impressive to anyone looking for someone with real interest in advancing in photography.

Your portfolio of photographs should be uniform in size—8 × 10, 11 × 14, or 16 × 20 inches—and clean and varied in subject matter. A professional folder from some art or office supply store that you use to carry your photographs mounted on mount boards will be professional in appearance. Be sure your prints are spotted carefully. Do not have ragged or crooked borders on your sample prints. Trim the borders off if you must use prints in this condition. In addition, do not put large lettering and your name on the front of your prints.

For appointments with commercial studios and company photographic departments, you should have some views showing products, buildings, equipment, furniture, fashions, automobiles, and groups of people and things. Your work should include close-up, medium-range, and long-distance views. Transparencies should be mounted in transparent vinyl-pocketed sheets for viewing over a light table. If arrangements can be made ahead of time, you may decide to put your 35mm transparencies in a carousel-type projector tray. Whatever you do, select very few examples of your work. Don't overwhelm your interviewer with a large number of photographs. Pictures of your little brother and sister are not impressive.

Don't depend on the judgment of your own family and friends for selecting the photographs to use and show to get a job. Take your portfolio of photographs and slides to some highly respected professional photographer and ask him or her for help and advice. Most recognized photographers will find time to help a young, eager photographer get started.

ATTENDING CONVENTIONS

If you possibly can, attend a photographic convention in your community, state, or province in order to show your samples and seek professional advice. You would not have to stay overnight if costs would be prohibitive and time would be limited. Drive to the convention and back the same day or for one evening. Take your sample photographs, or slides, and a list of notes to get opinions. At a convention, you would be able to get several good opinions from name photographers, as well as be able to see displays of professional photographs. Ask other photographers about certain photographs on display and what they think are the outstanding features of some of the photographs hanging in the exhibition. Take your camera along to make exposures of the award-winners and other prints that appeal to you so that you can take them back home to analyze and study. Just be sure that you use the exposures you make at the convention only for your own knowledge and not for any other purpose.

Whether or not you are a member of the photography group holding the convention will make no difference. Professional photographers are usually all around the hotel or convention hall, and the photographic exhibition is hung where it can be viewed by the public. If you are sincere and have a strong enough desire to see and hear a certain name photographer talk, you should have no trouble convincing an officer or board member to allow you to attend a particular program. There are usually student or associate memberships available that would not be too costly.

Bulletin boards for "help wanted" cards are usually on display at most photography conventions. Be sure to check this opportunity for finding employment. Post your name, address, and phone number. Also talk to as many photographic department managers and studio owners as possible.

KNOCKING ON DOORS

"Knocking on doors" is a fast way to get acquainted and learn of employment possibilities in photographic departments. Check the Yellow Pages of the phone book for a list of photographic establishments, and go to the placement bureau of your college or trade school, should you be a student or graduate. These are good sources to find out the places to call on for possible employment. Be sure to ask each person with whom you talk if he or she can recommend a company with a job opening.

Being aggressive, persistent, and enthusiastic about seeking employment will be to your advantage. If you have a portfolio of photographs, take them along in case you are asked to show samples. Leave your name, address, and telephone number—typed or written neatly on a plain white card—with the department manager or person interviewing you.

WRITING APPLICATION LETTERS

Letter writing should be used as your last resort in getting a photographic job. Naturally, there would be no other way, other than the cost of telephone conversations, or perhaps use of the Internet, to apply for positions in other cities or states where time and expense would rule out direct contact. Writing effective letters of application is a skill in itself. Prepare a letter on plain, white, 8 1/2 × 11 writing paper, preferably typewritten or word processed, giving information in separate paragraphs on the type of position wanted, education, experience, professional and community memberships, references, and personal information. Keep the letter simple, neat, and to the point, avoiding the use of "I" as much as possible. Again, seeking advice from someone more expert in letter writing would be a smart move on your part. Take a draft letter, written to the best of your ability, to someone in your school, church, or business to check and get helpful suggestions for improving its effectiveness. Your school principal, counselor, or English teacher, or a secretary in a large business could be helpful. There also are a number of books on resume and letter writing available at your local library or bookstore.

When you are satisfied that you have prepared the most effective application possible, there are a number of sources available for obtaining a list of places to send the letters. Your best bet for this list is the telephone company office or a large library. Ask your telephone company to let you see telephone directories of the cities in which you think you would like to live and work—then look under "photography" and "photographic establishments" in the Yellow Pages for places to write. Ask your local librarian for the latest *Directory of Professional Photography,* published annually by the Professional Photographers of America, Inc., and the *Membership Directory* of the National Press Photographers Association, Inc. If you are not able to obtain these two directories in your library, phone or visit some of the professional photographers listed in the phone book. Ask if they are NPPA or PPofA members and borrow a directory long enough to copy some names of persons to write to.

USING ADVERTISING TO GET EMPLOYMENT

If you wish to place classified advertisements for employment, here are some addresses of publications to write to for costs and deadline dates. Address your inquiries to the Advertising Department.

American Cinematographer
    1782 North Orange Drive
    Los Angeles, CA 90028

Editor and Publisher
    11 West Nineteenth Street
    New York, NY 10011-4234

Industrial Photography
    445 Broad Hollow Road
    Melville, NY 11747

News Photographer (c/o NPPA)
    1446 Conneaut Avenue
    Bowling Green, OH 43402

Photo Marketing
    3000 Picture Place
    Jackson, MI 42901

The Professional Photographer
    57 Forsyth Street
    Atlanta, GA 30303

The Rangefinder
    1313 Lincoln Boulevard
    P.O. Box 1703
    Santa Monica, CA 90406

SPE Journal and Service Notes
    6535 South Dayton Street
    Englewood, CO 80209

Studio Photography
    445 Broad Hollow Road
    Melville, NY 11747

These same publications are sources for finding "help wanted" advertisements. You could answer some of these ads before spending money on advertising. Also check the "help wanted" advertisements in your daily and nearby big city newspapers. One never knows for sure where the best opportunity lies for the future. Try them all.

In each state there are photography magazines, trade journals, bulletins, and mailing pieces sent regularly to members by state and large city professional photographers' associations. These are close-to-home publications with advertisements for help that receive good response because the publications are quickly and easily read. To find out about them, you would have to contact a company photographer or a studio owner for back issues or request that the next issue be saved for you.

ADVANTAGES OF A CAREER IN PHOTOGRAPHY

Photography as a profession can offer immense personal enjoyment and satisfaction. You can use it for the enjoyment of your whole family—while on vacations, in your home, during spare time, in another business, as a hobby, and on your job.

Photography includes some lucrative fields in which a darkroom and studio are not even necessary. Picture-postcard views as well as calendar and color brochure scenes can be photographed, then processed by labs in business for this type of work. All the photographer has to do is make the photographs, have a lab process the transparencies, show the proofs or transparencies to the customer, write the order, and deliver it to the printer for completion. There are several postcard printers who can furnish details on this type of business.

Students in thousands of schools are photographed for ID cards or yearbooks, and the work is sent to finishing plants to complete. The photographer photographs the students, sends the films away for processing, delivers or mails the finished prints to the schools, and collects the money—all without the use of a darkroom or studio. This is a highly specialized field and should be attempted only after thorough investigation.

Photography of individuals and family groups in homes and at summer resorts without darkroom facilities has become a lucrative business for many successful studio operations. Either the studio's own lab or some other, independent color finishing plant completely finishes the images for the photographer who made them. The completed orders are delivered later in person or by C.O.D. mail or express delivery. A deposit at the time of the sitting, or when the proofs are shown, is usually the practice, with the balance due on delivery of the finished order. Practice has proven that this type of operation works best when done as a full-time operation or in connection with a well-regarded photographic establishment.

The recent development of new techniques such as digital photography also has made it possible to view computer images instead of traditional proofs before making selections. This results in less waste of time and resources.

Good public relations and the character of people working in the photographic field are also important. As in most other professions, an increasing number of dedicated members in professional photography associations are campaigning to improve the principles of conduct governing individuals and group operations.

Flexibility is a key asset for any photographer. Peter Gowland has reminisced on occasions how he photographed weddings, made passport photos, and took anything he could get while he developed his flourishing, nationally known photography business. A well-known portrait photographer, who built a multimillion-dollar business, got started in photography while working as a street car conductor. A freelance commercial photographer roams the world furnishing photographs for travel agencies, airlines, passenger ships, magazines, and advertising agencies. He moved from San Francisco to Hawaii, where he is now based. Any number of success stories could be mentioned to illustrate opportunities in this field.

Photography is a field in which initiative, enthusiasm, creativity, and long hours can be rewarded with professional recognition, tremendous personal satisfaction, and just about any amount of money you want. Laziness, indifference, negative attitudes, sloppiness, and looking for an easy way out are the characteristics that will surely lead to failure in photography.

Other chapters in this book cover the varied fields of specialization, general photography opportunities, and how well each pays. Read these chapters, check your local library for photo publications, and talk with as many photographers as you can manage to meet—then make up your mind whether to go all the way in choosing photography as a lifetime profession. If you do decide that photography is for you, and you have most of the qualities mentioned, you will never regret your decision.

EARNING POTENTIAL

How much a photographer earns, in terms of dollars and cents, is the most difficult question to answer in this book. It is like answering the question: How much is creativity worth?

Estimates of salaries and wages in the photographic field vary considerably. Even current sources of information contain data that were compiled at least one to two years earlier.

Information mentioned on these pages has been obtained from a variety of reliable references. Most dollar amounts are averages, so actual low- and high-end salaries are much different than the dollars mentioned. Salaries also will vary by geographic region and be affected by changes in the economy in general. However, the following information will serve as a point of reference and will give the reader an idea of the fluctuations in earnings in photography.

Apprentice-beginners generally begin at minimum wage while getting started as all-around helpers in portrait, commercial, or similar studios. About $6 per hour or slightly more than $12,000 a year would be common, depending on the individual's qualifications and the size of the firm or city. If the opportunity to work as an apprentice under a photographer with a good reputation is offered, it would be wise to seriously consider taking the job primarily for the experience and guidance. Some students will accept this type of employment for part-time work while continuing their formal education.

After a few years of practical on-the-job experience, industrial photographers employed by corporations would have an advantage over employees of private studios because there are usually better fringe benefits and more frequent reviews for salary increases. Photo lab technicians doing processing and printing are now being given the same pay consideration as photographers' assistants with similar experience. Exceptionally talented and dedicated employees usually are recognized by their employers quickly and often receive incentive increases in pay. The degree of success you and your company enjoy also will have a bearing on your pay scale and the amount of increases, or bonuses, you receive.

Large firms with photographic studios tend to pay better than commercial or portrait studios. A person with a two-year or four-year degree in photography will have a better chance of obtaining a position than a person with similar experience and no degree.

Portrait studios tend to be owned and managed by one person but frequently have other family members working there. Sometimes there are some part-time or full-time additional photographers to help out in busy seasons.

Independent photographers and freelancers have the broadest range of incomes. The sheer majority of them probably earn only enough to make a modest living. But, they stay in business because they enjoy the freedom of being their own bosses and being able to, within reason, say yes or no to any assignment. There are a number of photographers who have made a name for themselves and can command very high fees for any assignment they choose to accept.

Magazine Photographs

Attempting to provide an approximation of the value of a photograph published in a magazine is difficult since there are so many variances. Some publications receive only small local distribution, others are regional, while the most widely circulated publications receive national distribution. The total circulation of a magazine is one of the primary criteria for establishing a print price, as is the size and location of the photograph used in print. Inside editorial usage seldom pays much, while any advertising usage of a picture will normally command top-dollar return for the photographer.

A small reproduction of a picture used to illustrate a story or article will naturally receive far less attention, and payment, than an eye-catching photo used on the cover. Cover photos rightfully receive the most pay, especially those used on newsstand publications, which depend on attracting the attention of shoppers and enticing them to purchase that issue of the magazine. An exclusive, unique, or rare photograph, especially one of a news event or some unusual happening that nobody else was able to photograph, will command a much higher price than a merely attractive or outstanding photo that anybody could have the opportunity to make. In the 1980s, one photographer made thousands of dollars for his dramatic photographs of the Mount St. Helens volcanic eruption—but he almost lost his life in the process of making those pictures!

One photographic magazine that is available on the newsstand nationwide currently pays about $400 per full color page. Another offers $50 to $200 per black-and-white photo. Large-circulation (or distribution) magazines pay the most, while controlled, low-circulation magazines that number their readers at 50,000 or fewer will pay considerably less for a similar photo.

One-time use rights are normally stipulated with the sale of any photo, so the picture is merely "leased" for this one use only. In actuality, one photo can be resold many times for use in different publications if it is unusual or attention-commanding. Thus, the income derived from rare or especially interesting pictures can continue for years. Conversely, sometimes a picture is sold outright, with all rights going to the buyer, who gains full control over its use. For this type of sale, a higher payment should be contracted since the photographer no longer owns the picture after the sale. There are other types of image rights that apply to photographs and their publication, but we will not go into detail about them.

A good source of information about markets for photographs is:

Photographers Market
  Writer's Digest Books
  F&W Publications
  1507 Dana Avenue
  Cincinnati, OH 45207

Photographs As Art

In the 1980s, photographs rapidly became more recognized as a form of art by museums, corporations, banks, galleries, and individual collectors. Along with this recognition, the prices commanded for outstanding photographs by well-known photographers also rose dramatically. This trend has continued in recent years.

Controversy accompanied the 1989 and 1990 national exhibitions of the work of photographer Robert Mapplethorpe, who died of AIDS in 1989. As a result, prices for his photographs, some of which critics have labeled obscene, doubled or tripled, with one self-portrait print selling for close to $40,000.

Recent photography sales at auction houses such as Sotheby's and Christie's, and at some prominent New York City galleries, have resulted in sales of photographs much in excess of their estimated value. Some photos even sold for up to triple the estimates, with some top-quality prints made by Alfred Stieglitz during his lifetime selling in a group of twenty-one for a record $396,000. A self-portrait of Paul Outerbridge sold for $99,000. Even the asking prices for prominent living photographers' prints currently are running at about ten times what was commonly asked as recently as the 1980s.

Quality photographs made by early photographers, especially those from a limited edition and signed, are becoming good investments. This does not imply that every photograph could potentially have such a high value, but outstanding examples of recognized master photographers are finally receiving the recognition and respect deserved by pioneers of the medium. Current sales trends show that considerable money can be made by creative, reliable photographers who can consistently produce top-quality results under a wide variety of circumstances.

CHAPTER 4

COMMERCIAL PHOTOGRAPHY

Separating the type of subjects or activities done by the commercial, portrait, or industrial photographer is difficult. There is a natural overlapping of each category. Even the equipment used can be similar, if not identical. In general, the commercial photographer photographs inanimate objects or things while the portrait photographer is more involved with people. Many smaller studios have only one or two photographers who wear many hats and produce quality images of things and people for their clients.

Commercial photographs produce images of many subjects. Typical would be:

construction and architecture
real estate
sales meetings
conventions
trade shows
golf tournaments
sailing, automobile, and other races
banquets
store and mall displays
fashion and clothing
manufactured items

These photographs might be used for publicity brochures or ads, web pages, company publications, catalogs, business and trade publications, display or wall decor, or postcards. The photographs record events or things for advertising, sales and promotional activities, and public relations for the client.

The commercial photographer is, in effect, a salesperson through photographs. Since he or she will be called upon to photograph a variety of subjects, the photographer must be versatile, quick to understand how the product works in order to photograph it intelligently, and able to exercise ingenuity. Learning all about a client's products and operation is important in order to hold an account for a long period of time. With this knowledge, the photographer can make photographs that will do a better job of selling the customer's products. Being able to tell the company's story photographically in a more imaginative way than other photographers is a priceless talent, and one that will hold accounts and bring increased business.

Commercial photography, however, is not the field for an up-and-coming photographer who wishes to take the time to do art photography. Commercial photography requires working under pressure. Sometimes it means being on call day and night, Sundays, and even holidays. Most jobs the commercial photographer undertakes have a rigid deadline.

Time is of the essence in commercial photography, and one of the photographer's most valuable commodities is fast service. The photographer must be ready to go at a moment's notice. It is not unusual for the photographer to answer the phone, receive a request from a customer, and be on the way to the assignment in a few minutes. Often photographers take the assignment in the afternoon and deliver the finished prints early the next morning. Because time is such a vital factor in commercial photography, some photographers maintain a complete set of equipment in their cars ready to go at all times. Failure to give speedy and dependable service has probably been responsible for more lost business than any other cause in commercial photography.

Commercial photographers range from the small-town business person who also does some portraits to the celebrated big-city illustrator who receives several thousand dollars for a single photograph. Although the latter gets high fees, the expenses are considerable. The photographer needs a good deal of working space, which means high rental, an extensive assortment of equipment, and complete set-building facilities, to mention but a few examples. Because the pictures one is assigned to make are often used in costly advertisements, clients are willing to pay the high fee of the prominent photographer, confident that he or she will produce an effective photograph. They cannot afford to take chances with the high cost of the advertising space, deadlines, model fees, and other expenses. Much depends on the effectiveness, that is, on the selling power, of the picture.

Obviously, it takes a long time to reach the level of the large commercial studios, most of which are located in the big cities, where important accounts have offices.

The majority of commercial studios do a general business—anything that comes along. As indicated previously, a commercial photographer may be called upon to photograph anything from banquets to window displays, from glassware to fashion, from passport photos to publicity pictures for magazines and newspapers. The tendency, however, is to specialize in one field, such as food or fashion, jewelry, furniture, and so on.

Some commercial photography studios specialize in architectural photography. Photography for catalogs is yet another popular specialization. Specialization is usually highly individualized. The photographer-owner does most of the work, with the help of assistants. There are also career opportunities in commercial photography studios for stylists—those who are responsible for details such as selecting props, dressing the set, and putting finishing touches on models' clothing, and for sales representatives and business managers. Of course, many laboratory technicians are needed.

Some of the best creative photography is being done in the fashion field, which calls for a combination of the artist and fashion expert, as well as a sharp eye for significant detail and the ability to portray the fashion product attractively.

ADVANTAGES AND DISADVANTAGES

In the event the commercial photographer plans to go into business for her- or himself, it would be wise to consider some of the disadvantages of this area of photography. There are long hours, last-minute rush assignments, deadline pressures, large investments in equipment, and the risks that any person takes when going into a business. Some of these disadvantages would not exist, however, if the photographer is an employee of a large commercial studio.

On the other hand, there are compensations and much personal satisfaction in this type of photography. It takes a particular business acumen to operate a successful commercial photography studio. There is the challenge of dealing directly with other successful businesspeople who come to you with various assignments. In addition, no two jobs are alike. This also makes for a great deal of challenge and diversification to the work. A chance to travel and the opportunity to learn firsthand about many different types of businesses and products are other advantages of commercial photography.

The financial return for a commercial photography business can be very lucrative through the years as you help to increase the demand for your clients' products. Usually, eye-appealing photographs that do a good job of selling are the results of one or more alert photographers in an organization. If one account shows a steady business improvement—through the effectiveness of good photographs—it is more than likely that the same will prove true with all the other accounts. In this way, your photographic business will show a steady increase with an increasing number of new accounts. The goal is to develop a style of photography that makes companies and agencies come to you for outstanding photographs. It can be an endless chain of growth.

ILLUSTRATIVE OR ADVERTISING PHOTOGRAPHY

Selling or "telling the story" of a company's product for use in national advertisements, newspapers, magazines, and for some TV commercials is the job of the illustrative photographer. Going through the pages of almost any national magazine, you should be immediately aware of the high quality of the many ads. It is the photograph's purpose in such an ad to influence the consumer visually to purchase the item—the success or failure of the ad is reflected in a company's sales figures. The advertiser usually spends an enormous sum of money for these ads, and illustrative photography is a very highly competitive field requiring the latest approaches and techniques in photography. Creativity, however, is the main ingredient needed by the photographer in order to build a business and reputation in this particular classification of photography. He or she will work with other talented individuals, such as artists, advertising managers, and art directors. Because they are creative thinkers, illustrative photographers will find working with people who are thinking up new ideas to be interesting and exciting.

The key to illustrative photography is creativity, so there is no single approach the photographer can take to ensure success. Very often the illustrative photographer will work from an artist's sketch of what is to be portrayed in a photograph. Or, he or she will be expected to interpret some idea or concept as an eye-catching sales illustration. At other times, the ideas for photographs may have to be researched by reading and looking at illustrations in libraries, museums, or art galleries. An interior decorator, food economist, or other highly specialized person or technical advisor from another field may have to be consulted in completing the photography setup.

The illustrator often is paid to produce an illustration completely different from anything used before and that bears no resemblance to the competitor's sales presentation or advertisements. Often a particular type of model may play such an important part in the illustration that it could easily take several days looking for just the right subject that was originally conceived in the mind of the client or advertising sales executive. Going through modeling agency files can be quite time-consuming because of the need to locate a fresh new face never seen before in other advertisements.

Getting the proper backgrounds and settings for certain products to be photographed can at times be difficult. The cost can be enormous, too. In some cases, the photo illustrator has been known to take props and a staff of assistants to an out-of-the-way island or some other remote place to do exactly what the client ordered. The matter of a few hundred dollars expense one way or the other is not important to an agency that is seeking an eye-catching ad to run in *Time, Newsweek, National Geographic, Reader's Digest, The Smithsonian,* or some other national publication. Such an ad can be a full-page spread or a double-page spread costing thousands of dollars to run in a single issue of the magazine.

Several photo illustrators also have had great success breaking into TV commercial production—which can be an even more lucrative and fast-paced field.

MEETINGS AND CONVENTIONS

In convention cities and resort areas, a specialized field of photography has been developed by some studios. They photograph convention or meeting participants in small and large groups, in formal and informal "at work" situations. Now, with the decentralization of meeting facilities, nearly every hotel and motel can accommodate meetings of organizations and companies. In addition to group photographs, the enterprising photographer will take pictures of workshops in action, awards presentations, new officer installations, and trade show exhibition booths.

Another profitable business can be built upon the growing need for audiovisual presentations, from a simple slide show to a multimedia production. Many modern hotels and motels are designed with built-in AV facilities, including arrangements for closed-circuit television programming. Along with the growing need for audiovisual programming will develop a body of experienced AV producers, script writers, programmers, and technicians. The growing need for visual material on Internet "websites" holds similar potential. The young person considering audiovisual or web page production as a career should be prepared to meet talented competition.

EQUIPMENT

Equipment requirements for a commercial photographer can vary considerably from those of photographers engaged solely in portraiture. The commercial photographer will be required to photograph anything from a photomicrographic specimen to the biggest building in the city from a helicopter. Thus, the commercial photographer may need a much greater financial outlay to start his or her business than the portrait or industrial person.

To have a complete studio, a minimum of $50,000 to more than $100,000 would be needed. The industrial photographer working for a company would have equipment furnished and geared to specific fields of coverage. The commercial photographer would have to own a car or even a station wagon, van, or truck. In all likelihood, this vehicle would be loaded with a good deal of equipment.

The commercial photographer needs a varied selection of cameras and lenses ready to go at a moment's notice. Cameras in the 8 × 10, 4 × 5, 2¼ × 2¼, and 35mm sizes all have uses on different jobs, along with an assortment of lenses suitable for each of them.

Commercial photographers rely on electronic flash for the variety of work they are expected to perform. Studio electronic flashes are not very portable; therefore, small portable electronic flashes are frequently used. Incandescent and quartz, as continuous light sources, also will be of great use for catalogs, magazines, and fashion publicity and advertising. Broad, even, diffused light from light banks and other soft light sources is popular today. You must educate yourself on unusual lighting sources so you will be prepared to handle any type of assignment.

A ground-floor or downtown location for a commercial studio would not be as important to the commercial photographer as it might be to the portrait photographer, who caters to a certain number of walk-in customers. However, the commercial photographer who has accounts with companies that manufacture large products, such as appliances, furniture, or automobiles, would need a large, ground-floor location with high ceilings and a side entrance for moving in these large products for photographing.

DARKROOM/LABORATORY

Jerry L. Cornelius of Cornelius Photography in Tulsa, Oklahoma, suggested that a commercial photographer should have darkroom equipment in the studio for fast service.

"The normal commercial customer cannot wait for work to be farmed out to a lab," said Cornelius. However, if at the start of your business venture you do not wish to process your own film and enlarge your own prints, you may want to contact one of the professional processing labs in your area and establish a good working rapport with the staff there. You can handle rush jobs even without your own darkroom if you have good connections at the lab.

If you do plan to furnish your own processing and finishing, then equipment such as washers, dryers, enlargers, and contact printers will be essential to give fast delivery of prints to your customers. Automatic processors for film and prints will be a must.

FREELANCE PHOTOGRAPHY

Freelance photographers work on their own instead of serving as employees of a business or nonprofit organization. Typically they work for a variety of clients.

Freelancers establish a point of operation where mail and phone calls may be collected and acknowledged wherever they may be working. In many cases, the freelancers' spouses act as business managers, and home is their base of operation. Sometimes both husband and wife are photographers, and they share correspondence and bookkeeping details. A telephone answering device or answering service is essential to the freelancer. E-mail is also helpful.

Most freelancers are "loners" and are on the go most of the time—that is, if they are in the top income bracket and their work and names have become prominent enough to make businesses, agencies, photo editors, and syndicates want their photographic services.

Some freelance photographers have their own darkrooms and spend time at the home base doing their own processing and printing, while others arrange with a studio to do their finishing.

Most successful freelancers arrange with custom laboratories to handle all their processing and printing. Even while the photographer is away on another assignment, instructions are sent in with the film to be processed, contact-printed, and delivered to the client. The client studies the contact sheets and indicates how the picture is to be cropped in the enlargement for the intended picture story or advertising layout.

Equipment needed by freelancers who cover assignments anywhere in the United States and out of the country can amount to a sizable investment, although they have to travel with the least possible amount of weight while on the road. Two or three 35mm camera bodies with wide-angle, normal, and long focal length lenses, a 4 × 5 view camera with assorted lenses, as well as a 120 size camera are a must in order to be prepared to handle a greater percentage of the jobs. Electronic flash equipment also is necessary.

There are many sources listing photo markets in which you may want to list your availability to do assignments. These same sources also can be consulted to sell your stock photos. A half-day spent in the reference department of your nearest large library making a list of the current market publications and companies that purchase outside photography will be profitable.

One of the better sources of photography sales possibilities is:

Working Press of the Nation
National Register Publishing
121 Chanlon Road
New Providence, NJ 07974

It includes a freelance guide to more than 4,000 of the nation's leading house magazines, listing magazine titles, editors, company names, and addresses, as well as photographic subjects and stock photography agencies.

Another book of interest to the beginner in freelance or stock photography sales is:

Photographer's Market
Writer's Digest Books
1507 Dana Avenue
Cincinnati, OH 45207

This book is updated each year with comprehensive listings of the photographic needs in a variety of categories and markets. *Sell and Re-Sell Your Photos,* by Rohn Engh, also is available from Writer's Digest Books. It provides sage advice on pricing, film, copyrights, taxes, recordkeeping, and other aspects of selling your photos nationwide by mail.

Stock picture agencies are always looking for fresh sources of quality photos. However, this is not a "get rich quick" type of photography. Unless you have a quite unusual and visually different photograph that will sell immediately, you should be prepared to furnish several hundred photographs, or slides, and possibly wait a year or more for any sales to develop. It is, however, a good source of extra income from photography, and should be seriously considered by many individuals.

There are several hundred stock agencies all over the United States and Canada. Most handle color and black-and-white pictures of a wide variety of photographic subjects including people, business, scenic, architecture, and cities, while others specialize in topics such as sports, nature, agriculture, glamour, food, news, or history. Several agencies you might want to contact are:

Archive Photos
    530 West Twenty-fifth Street
    New York, NY 10001

Stockworks
    11936 West Jefferson Boulevard
    Culver City, CA 90230

Ro-MA Stock
    1003 South Los Robos Avenue
    Pasadena, CA 91106-4332

The Stock Solution
    307 West 200 South
    Salt Lake City, UT 84101

Making contacts with the art directors and photo editors of advertising agencies, photo syndicates, newspapers, and magazines is a move in the right direction. After the freelance photographer has established several accounts, he or she can become selective or specialize in a specific type of photography.

AERIAL PHOTOGRAPHY

Some photographers and companies specialize almost exclusively in the science of photogrammetry—aerial photography—and there are enough of these companies to warrant the organization of an association known as the American Society of Photogrammetry, which sponsors annual conventions and seminars for studying and advancing the work of aerial photography. Special planes, with cameras installed into the planes' bottoms, make up a vital part of their expensive and specialized equipment. The planes are used for mapping and surveying operations throughout the United States and foreign countries.

Many aerials are made by the general photography studios found in both small towns and cities. Rented airplanes, planes belonging to friends, and all kinds of cameras are used in doing the photography. Where aerial cameras like those used in the different branches of the armed forces are not available, any format hand-held camera, dependent upon the subject matter and quality required by the client, can make acceptable aerial photographs.

Most of the large-scale photogrammetry work is done for county, state, and federal governments, as well as for companies holding large acreages of land and for foreign governments. Photographs of most state land are on file for use in determining where new charts of highways, pipelines, and rivers will be done. Also, the heights of mountains and depths of valleys and canyons are studied and measured from these aerial photographs. Pollution of rivers and lakes as well as the effects of fires and diseases of forests and crops can be detected through the use of aerial photographs.

Aerial photographs also are used for planning large-scale projects such as the locating of airport sites, railroad systems, power lines, and so on. Other projects involve surveying crop conditions and timberland and recording changes in rivers, shorelines, and mountains where erosion is at work. Still other airview subject matter includes factories, homes, country clubs, housing projects, and shopping centers. Likely markets for such pictures are the owners of the properties, real estate agents, local officials, colleges, yacht clubs, airports, and newspapers.

Aerial photography is a specialization in which photographers can earn a regular living. Aside from jobs with airlines, employment opportunities can be found in government work and on the staffs of large aerial survey companies. Interpreting photographs of the earth's resources taken from space is a field for future photographers with scientific training and backgrounds.

Lyndon B. Johnson once said, "If we had no justification other than the photography, it would be worth ten times more than the $35–$40 billion the U.S. has spent to date on its space program." Many Americans would agree with him.

Some excellent thoughts about aerial photography appeared in *The Professional Photographer* magazine. Harper Leiper, past president of the Professional Photographers of America, wrote:

> There is money to be made in aerial photography but you cannot make it on aerial photography alone. You've got to be doing several things and have income from all of them.
>
> It takes time to build a file of stock aerials. But if you have a good system, they are money makers. Our stock file is about 7,000 11 × 14 prints. They account for about a third of our gross now. It's the easiest profit you'll ever make. We have a big map indexed to the file, and the customer just comes in and looks up the area on

which he wants an aerial. We charge more for older prints, in increments of ten years.

If a customer purchases an aerial from our stock file and wants more copies of it, he doesn't have to pay the basic fee over again. He can get as many as he wants at our regular reprint rates. Many times they do request 25 to 50 copies.

Every three years I do a City Strip to make a record of the populated areas of Houston. I go to 10,000 feet in a fixed-wing aircraft and, using a handheld camera, shooting at about an 80° angle along a predetermined path, I strip the town at 100 mph. I make an exposure every 30 seconds, and I find that these overlap enough to give me a complete picture of the city.

CHAPTER 5

PORTRAIT PHOTOGRAPHY

A good beginning point for many photographers is outdoor portrait photography. All that is required is a camera, film, and a willing subject. The typical subject of most amateurs' cameras is a family member, friend, pet, or neighborhood child. Naturally, each subject—except the pet—wants to see the finished pictures. If they like them, they will want extra prints to keep. The photographer often is also anxious to see what the photographs look like enlarged. If the subjects can afford it, they may contribute to the cost of film and printing. Thus a budding business is born. But, the next major question is, can you continue doing this and produce a regular income?

What to charge for photography is often one of the most difficult decisions to make in the profession. In the beginning it is just a guess, and—believe it or not—some photographers go through a lifetime in the business without being sure they have been fair with their prices. A great number of studios are operated with the photograph's spouse and the assistance of other members of the family. They sometimes work endless hours without being paid a set salary or even being on the payroll.

As the demand increases for photographs from amateurs, their interest in learning more about the profession increases. Reading more magazines and books, visiting other photographers, and joining photography associations helps in making the decision to go into the business full-time.

At this point, it is wise to think twice and get further counsel on what to do. The important thing to give thought to is whether you have enough training and skill to make sufficient progress in the portraiture field or whether you should first get additional training through workshops, short courses, or as a student in a photography school.

Another consideration is to weigh the advantages of working for an established studio for three or four years to learn the techniques of the business. Most of the older, well-known photographers got their start by serving as assistants or apprentices in studios. Today, making the choice is a bit more involved, with so many short courses in every field of photography. In addition, there are good academic courses in high schools, community colleges, and universities, as well as in trade and correspondence schools. Then, too, there is more specialization today than ever before and many new advances because of improved materials and equipment. Technical advances and increasing interest in fine color portraiture will make for continued growth and expansion in this field.

ADVANTAGES AND DISADVANTAGES

The field of portrait photography can be particularly appealing for several reasons. One plus is the control the photographer has over the use of his or her time. This is probably the only photographic field in which this advantage can be controlled to any great extent. Portrait photographers can schedule sittings for a time convenient to themselves. They can even refer sittings to another studio. A commercial or freelance photographer would have to take the chance of losing an account of many years' standing, running into thousands of dollars, if he or she were not available to do a certain job at a certain time, day or night. Industrial photographers and others working on a salary could not take off anytime they wanted to because they would not have any control over the policy concerning their working hours and vacations.

Another reason that makes the portrait studio a greater attraction as a private business venture is that the photographer's spouse can become a partner and be valuable help in keeping the business established. Over 90 percent of all portrait studios were started as husband-and-wife operations. It usually works out that one does the photographing, processing, and printing, while the other handles the retouching, spotting, and bookkeeping.

A portrait studio's financial success cannot be judged by its decor or by the number of employees. Nor should it be belittled because it is a family business. A large percentage of such business teams net more take-home pay than many studios with a larger number of employees and higher gross incomes. Most of the larger studios with large staffs, high gross incomes, and big overheads are located in the cities, whereas the family studios are usually found in the suburbs and smaller communities.

Despite the philosophy that if you don't keep pace with progress you will fall behind, there are many small, happily established businesses that prefer avoiding additional work and responsibility and make no effort to grow bigger. On the other hand, there are those who do everything in their power to become large businesses and outdo their competitors. In many cases, growth is necessary in order to keep contracts and maintain an established business. Computerization has become a necessity today with the large portrait studios that sign contracts for photographing senior classes and undergraduates in a large number of schools. Some studios have become such large operations that traveling studios built into trailers are being used to photograph students in several states.

It is possible to build a portrait business into almost any type of business you want, small or large, with growth potential, being able to arrange your time for long vacations, getting enjoyment from the use of boats and summer cottages, having memberships in ski and golf clubs, and the like. Remember, too, that a proportionate share of hard knocks (failures and lean years) go along with something that has as many pleasures as operating one's own business.

STUDIO LOCATION

If you have decided to go into photography full-time after making pictures for a few years, working to get experience in a good portrait studio for three or four years, or finishing a photography course in one of the fine photography trade schools, colleges, or universities, you will need to decide where to locate your establishment.

Most portrait studios are started in a small community or particular section of a city with potential portrait business. Many studios depend largely on getting a good part of the yearly senior portraits from the community's high schools. After doing the senior class portraits in a school, there is a tendency to add another school and then another as the years go on.

Besides adult portraits and high school senior portraits, baby portraits and wedding photography are important segments of a successful portrait studio. Some studios specialize in portraiture of children by orienting all their promotion, decoration, equipment, and presentation in this direction. In the past few years, there has been an increase in the photographing of family groups, pets, and children in the home atmosphere or outdoors in environmental settings. Large dye transfer and other color print finishes, sold in expensive, museum-type frames, have been responsible for building an increasing number of portrait studio businesses into more than $100,000 endeavors.

Initially, you will have to decide whether you want to start working from your home, build a studio, or lease a building. Location of your business and studio should be of prime consideration. It should be located relatively close to a busy shopping area with ample parking nearby. Your building should be large enough to have a pleasant reception area and adequate studio space for both individual and group portraits.

Seek the best location available that will be within your estimated operating budget. Only you will know what this should be, after talking to other professional photographers and your banker. By all means, check first on your local zoning ordinance to see if the law permits you to build or rent property for a photography studio.

Although you may start by renting space, it would be advisable to keep in mind that you may someday, after building a successful photography business, want to own the location for your business. Parking, a good display window, and a place for a sign are other necessities in order to make a speedier beginning in business. As your business grows, parking space will become more and more important. Take into consideration, also, that the farther you are from a main street or downtown shopping area, the more you will have to spend on advertising and promotion to keep your name and location constantly in view of the buying public.

It will be worth your time to check on the potential growth of the area in which you expect to start, as well as the tax history of the community. Leasing with an option to buy after two or three years is something else to consider. The general appearance and layout of the building you use, along with the adjoining properties, should be appealing to customers. A visit with real estate agents to discuss what you are looking for would prove helpful in gaining valuable knowledge before making a final decision.

Your ability and willingness to learn and to work long, hard hours to get a business going are crucial no matter where you are located. An artistic nature and the ability to produce high-quality photographs, which will win awards in competition with other professional photographers, will attract an increasing number of customers to your business, even though your location may not be the most convenient one available.

BUSINESS COMPETITION

All successful people and businesses face competition. This should be met with an open mind and a favorable attitude. Competition is not limited to others in the portrait photography business. It can be the jeweler, drugstore, gift shop, or TV and appliance dealer down the street. Each family has just so much money to spend after paying for food, clothing, and housing. And every other business is after the same extra dollars that will be spent for luxuries. It then becomes necessary in order to be successful in the portrait field to make use of promoting, selling, publicizing, advertising, and presenting your photographs. Making the buying public conscious of your studio and desirous of owning what you have to sell is what will make the real difference in the amount of sales you total up at the end of the year.

Other kinds of competition you will have to be prepared for are price-cutting, premium offers, contests, telephone solicitation, door-to-door sales, and gimmicks of all kinds to attract portrait photography customers to competitors.

Fortunately, with the higher cost of traveling, necessity of better bookkeeping, requirements for business licenses, existence of professional photography organizations, and greater number of academically trained photographers, there seem to be fewer "fly-by-nighters" today than in years past. Larger, automated businesses are doing most of the volume of portrait business in this country today.

In response to increased competition, a portrait studio in Alabama operates a wedding shop adjacent to the studio. Wedding dresses, bridesmaids' dresses, and renting of tuxedos are featured, along with a catering service and gowns for mothers of the bride and groom. Special discounts are given to the bride on her wedding pictures with the purchase of her dress. The addition of a wedding shop has substantially increased the studio's wedding photography business.

EQUIPMENT

Most portrait studios use 120 roll film cameras with a medium telephoto lens (about 180mm) to photograph individuals. Of course, shorter focal length lenses also will be needed for photographing couples or groups. Outdoor, environmental photography is very popular today for both high school seniors and family groups. Medium-format, 120 roll film cameras also are used for this type of portraiture outside the studio. More compact and portable 35mm cameras are seldom used for professional portraiture. This is because the 24 × 36mm (35mm film) negative is too small for retouching easily. The 120 film cameras produce an image three to five times larger. It is not only easier to retouch, but also can be enlarged to produce much bigger wall display prints.

A wheeled monopod studio stand for inside work and a sturdy tripod outdoors are essential for producing top-quality images with the larger, heavier, medium-format cameras. Newer models of these cameras offer optional automatic exposure and motorized film advance features. This automation gives the photographer more time to devote to capturing memorable poses of the subjects.

Lighting

Portrait studio lighting is primarily electronic flash for photographing people of all ages. The bright, but extremely short-duration, light is excellent for capturing the subject, yet it remains cool. Years ago, continuous light sources, such as tungsten or quartz lamps, were more common. But the portrait subject often became uncomfortable under the hot lighting.

Studio electronic flash units are AC powered and bulky. Often they are on wheeled stands that telescope for height adjustment. Also available are overhead rail lighting systems that suspend the light heads from the ceiling. This minimizes the clutter of stands and cords often found in portrait studios. Portrait lights tend to have large reflectors, twelve to sixteen inches in diameter. They have movable barn doors and diffusion screens for simple adjustment of the quality of light produced. Each light has its own incandescent modeling light, which makes it simple to position the lights to produce the exact intensities and shadows desired for each individual's unique facial features. The intensity of the modeling lights varies to correspond with the intensity of the flash itself. A minimum of four such lights, two floods and two spotlights, are needed for quality portraiture.

A soft, complimentary type of studio light frequently used for photographing women is the umbrella light. Most any studio light can be easily adapted to accept an umbrella. Other helpful studio accessories include adjustable-height posing tables, reflectors, and vignetting diffusers to place in front of the lens.

For candid coverage of weddings, bar mitzvahs, and other occasions, more portable cameras and lighting equipment are necessary. Small 35mm equipment is commonly used for these events since this type of camera is far more portable. Compact, powerful, battery-powered electronic flash units can be used on either automatic or manual to adequately light most events. For large groups, several additional flash units, with an electric-eye slave that syncs them with the camera flash, can be an asset in obtaining proper lighting.

Portable flash units are sometimes used for environmental portraiture. More often, white cardboard or fold-up cloth reflectors or umbrellas are carried to provide the additional fill light required in some outdoor situations. Sometimes black umbrellas are used to shade and produce more flattering diffused lighting.

Whether working indoors with artificial lighting or outdoors with natural light, the portrait photographer must always control the lighting so the subjects will look their best. Most individuals do not have their portrait made very often, so it is the photographer's responsibility to produce the best quality possible.

Processing

Although most portrait studios have a rudimentary darkroom on their premises, it frequently is equipped only for basic black-and-white processing and printing. Most portraits, other than press release views, are made on color negative film, and the resulting prints are color enlargements.

Most smaller-volume studios do not produce enough portraits, or have a large enough staff of employees, to justify doing their own color film and print processing in-house. Custom color processing labs are found everywhere today and often offer pick-up and delivery service to studios within a nominal driving distance. Even when using mail, or UPS service, round-trip to a color lab usually only takes about a week. So the added costs and skills necessary to install and operate a color processing lab are impractical. The advent of digital photography promises significant change in this area. Production of photos through the use of computers and color printers will become increasingly common and continues to grow more promising.

Smaller portrait studios today find that they must be able to do more than produce quality studio portraits to survive. Large-volume portrait studios operating out of mass merchandising stores provide tough competition on pricing. Independent studios must diversify and offer additional services to keep busy. Environmental portraiture, copy and restoration of old photographs, and framing are several common sidelines that can bring in additional business.

Many skills in addition to being able to adjust the lights and expose film correctly are needed. Some artistic skills for retouching color negatives and spotting prints are essential. Keeping detailed records and books for scheduling sittings, planning delivery of finished work, and all financial transactions must be done by somebody at the studio. Often the photographers and their spouses handle most of these tasks until the volume of work justifies hiring additional people.

Purchasing all-new equipment to start a portrait studio is expensive. This type of small business has an unusually high number of failures, so be cautious. Sometimes you can find an established studio that is for sale because the owner is retiring or moving. Purchasing an existing facility with most of the equipment you will need, and a list of customers, often can be the best way for a younger photographer to get started. Check the classified ads in the back of publications such as *The Professional Photographer, The Rangefinder,* and *Studio Photography* for current listings of studios and equipment for sale.

If you decide to open a studio of your own, try to have adequate capital to stay in business for a year or more with minimal additional income. It takes time to become established and pay all the monthly bills as well as have some left over for a salary for yourself.

Portraiture with the 35mm Camera

For each picture-making situation and for each photographer, there is a format that is appropriate to the creation of the ideal image. Alfred Eisenstadt, a pioneer in the use of the 35mm camera, was the first of many who responded to the particular possibilities of this format to make exciting, alive portraits.

The advantages of 35mm portraiture are:

- *Size.* The relatively small size of the camera means easy portability and availability for location and informal portraiture.
- *Flexibility.* The variety of lenses available, their easy interchangeability, and the greater number of exposures per loading encourage creative exploration.
- *Ease of use.* The relatively greater depth of field of shorter lenses means that photographs can be made with less light.

Print size (extreme enlargements) and quality used to be considered limitations of the 35mm format. However, today's materials and the capabilities that many laboratories have for the production of large prints have minimized these problems.

The 35mm camera can be used in a portrait studio in place of a view camera, but it is in environmental situations that the 35mm presents the greatest opportunities for unique portraiture. The subject can be actively involved with the photographer and can be captured on film as the real individual he or she is, without the dissimulation that often occurs in formal, camera-on-tripod situations. The photojournalistic portrait is an obvious example. Executive portraits appearing in annual reports and other corporate publications are often done with a 35mm camera, portraying people in actual situations to convey spontaneity and credibility. The 35mm is also a natural for informal portraits of children and the tool *par excellence* for character studies and travel photos.

One caution: A simple fun-and-games, "click-click" approach will produce only sloppy snapshots. The fundamental requirements of appropriate lighting, good composition, and control of the image are the same for 35mm and for larger formats. Even when unable to manipulate the subject, light, and location, the photographer must be aware of everything in the picture area. He or she also must be so familiar with the equipment that the mechanical aspects are automatic, permitting concentration on the esthetics of the picture and interaction with the subject in a natural manner. The results can be strong images—portraits full of life and reality.

REFERENCE SOURCES

It is difficult to give advice on photography without referring to the increasing number of valuable and inexpensive aids available through the Eastman Kodak Company. And, if you plan a sizable operation in photography, several companies provide assistance in planning your studio and processing facilities. Ask your photographic supply dealer or another professional photographer how to get in touch with one of these valuable friends.

Photographic supply salespersons, representing dozens of companies anxious to make new contacts for sales and service, are good sources of helpful information on where to get firsthand advice from the most successful people in the profession. The names of these men and women are easy to find. Just ask a professional photographer who has an established business location.

Reference is made again to the most valuable, up-to-date information source of all, the *Directory of Professional Photography,* published yearly by the Professional Photographers of America, Inc. The Buyers Guide section is a guide to leading businesses offering photographic goods and services to the industry. This same directory lists all the PPofA members' names, locations, and addresses. Write to the PPofA for current price and availability of the *Directory.*

Other publications targeted toward photography also publish buying information for their readers. See the list of publications in Appendix A for more information. An increasing amount of product information, including objective reviews, is also available on the Internet.

It is always a good idea to read as much as you can about the features of any type of photographic equipment prior to purchasing new items. Reading what publications have to say is a good practice for anybody who will be using the equipment.

CHAPTER 6

INDUSTRIAL PHOTOGRAPHY

Businesses and industrial concerns often have enough year-round photographic work to justify having internal photographic departments. (Departments range in size from one person to several hundred; they are usually related to the size of the company and its use of photography.) Sometimes the products photographed are so large, or secret, that the firm does not want outsiders to see the product. Uses of the photographs are many. They might be very technical, complex analysis photos for engineering research and development, records of processes and equipment, or publicity or advertising photos. All types of equipment are used: conventional color and black-and-white stills from 35mm to 8 × 10; high-speed analysis films; videotapes; stills made from digital cameras; motion pictures; slides and filmstrips; photoresist and high-contrast litho.

The industrial photographer is usually a very versatile individual. Assignments can include every aspect of commercial photography, as well as portrait and illustration. Characteristics of a good industrial photographer include:

- *Competence*—the industrial photographer must be an extremely good technician
- *Versatility*—to handle a large variety of assignments
- *Imagination*—to bring variety and interest to everyday assignments

JOB PREPARATION

The best qualification for obtaining a job in industrial photography is a degree from a recognized college or university. The course of study should include a large amount of technical photography, photo lab technology, and basic video, as well as the artistic and design courses. Experience in any kind of photography, in addition to training, is also a plus.

Most beginning jobs are specialized, such as processing and laboratory work, but advancement does require the ability to be flexible and versatile. Each company has its own unique photographic requirements, and most departments are specifically designed to meet these needs.

ADVANTAGES AND DISADVANTAGES

Working situations in industrial photography are quite different from those in commercial or portrait photography. Most companies keep a 40-hour week, and the hours are regular and predictable. However, last-minute overtime is common to get projects completed.

Most industrial photographers are paid on an hourly basis. Department managers and the top photographers are sometimes salaried. In general, the pay rates of industrial photographers are the best in the photographic field. In addition to salaries, many fringe benefits are usually provided. Company cars, pension and profit sharing, retirement benefits, paid vacations, hospitalization insurance, and sick leave are benefits that may be offered by large companies. Only some of these benefits would be available in the small photographic studios. There are often extensive travel opportunities, with all expenses paid. This is not as glamorous as it sounds. A photographer traveling worldwide alone has to contend with cases of equipment, customs, the possibility of illness in strange surroundings, and a hard schedule.

A major disadvantage of industrial photography would probably be slower advancement than you might find in a commercial photographic operation. Many companies have dress codes, and business dress is sometimes required. The hours that must be kept are strictly enforced, and people who do not have good on-time and attendance records usually don't last very long. In most companies, photography is not a full-time business, so the photographer may have less stature in the company than others who are directly involved in the production of a product.

All in all, though, the industrial or corporate photographer is usually well paid and enjoys good equipment and working conditions.

GETTING STARTED

There is no clear-cut, tried-and-true method of obtaining a position as an industrial photographer. Some of the methods are obvious, such as looking in newspapers or trade periodicals for help-wanted ads or knocking on doors at companies that have a photographic department. Registering with employment agencies also produces results occasionally. Most often, job openings are created by expanded workloads or replacing people who are leaving. Most people are hired through the company's personnel department. Many positions are filled through contacts made in local photographic associations and affiliates of the Professional Photographers of America.

CHAPTER 7

SCIENTIFIC AND TECHNICAL PHOTOGRAPHY

Scientific and technical aspects of photography are difficult to define, since they are diversified and include both picture-making and nonpicture-making skills and activities.

Picture-making aspects of this exciting, broad field include high-speed photography, lasers, electron microscopes, holograms, stroboscopes, high-speed film, video cameras, photomacrography, photomicrography, color photography, and color printing. An individual with a background and experience in this field (which normally requires advanced education plus considerable on-the-job training) could work primarily in nonpicture-making activities. These include technical writing, laboratory supervision, product development and testing, sales, or technical representation for manufacturers of photographic equipment and materials.

Academic training in this discipline is not available everywhere. The Rochester Institute of Technology offers both two-year A.A.S. and four-year B.S. degrees in imaging and photographic technology among the seven subject areas offered in undergraduate photographic courses. There are relatively few picture-making courses in this program; instead, it is dominantly science-engineering in orientation. The number of graduates is relatively small, but there is a considerable demand for individuals with this type of training, so graduates often receive high starting pay compared to other branches of photography.

Other schools and colleges offer courses in various aspects of scientific and technical photography; check catalogs or program brochures for details.

A random sampling of individuals doing technical photography work disclosed that there were more than 250 job titles that covered this aspect of photography.

SOCIETY FOR IMAGING SCIENCE AND TECHNOLOGY

According to the Society for Imaging Science and Technology, "There are two directions you can take in photographic sciences. You can work in the application of photography to the needs of industry, medicine, and government. Or you can carry out pure research aimed at the discovery and control of the basic elements of photography."

The Society for Imaging Science and Technology has several technical sections within its membership, concentrating on special areas of photography. Perhaps one of the following areas will be of interest to the young person considering photography as a career.

- *Applied Photography* deals with industrial, law enforcement, and general professional photographic systems.
- *Business Graphics* covers such areas as microfilming, COM (computer output microfilming), office copying systems, identification systems, and engineering drawing reproduction.
- *Photochemistry* covers the chemistry of photography, including sensitization, latent image development mechanisms, blemish or fading mechanisms, and the kinetics of photographic chemistry.
- *Electrophotography* covers the whole spectrum of electrostatic image formation, including image decay, sensitization of photoconductors, toning, and photoelectric phenomena.

- *Graphic Arts* is devoted to halftone systems, lithography and gravure, photochemical reproduction, phototypesetting, and prepress technology.
- *Image Evaluation* concentrates on sensitometry, densitometry, color and tone reproduction, information theory, lens evaluation, and photometry.
- *Scientific Photography* studies such advanced technologies as holography, photofabrication, high-speed photography, underwater and aerial photography, digital image processing, and medical photography.
- *Medical Radiography* is the somewhat more specialized section that deals with screen film systems, iconography, x-ray spectrum, and diagnostic and therapeutic radiography.
- *Photofinishing* covers all aspects of photofinishing operations. It includes everything from engineering and equipment to automated packaging and billing.
- *Processing Techniques* has its emphasis on the chemistry of processing, including the ecological aspects of processing.

For further information write to the Society for Imaging Science and Technology, 7003 Kilworth Lane, Springfield, VA 22151.

INTERNATIONAL SOCIETY FOR OPTICAL ENGINEERING

The broad range of subjects represented by the International Society for Optical Engineering is an indication of many more kinds of imaging a student may consider as a career:

Biomedical Research	Electronic Imaging
Cartography	Electro-optical Systems
Coherent Optics	Environmental Quality
Earth Resources	Fiber Optics Techniques

High-speed Photography	Optical Systems Design
Holography	Pattern Recognition
Image Enhancement	Photo-optical Materials
Image Processing	Photographic Data Recording
Infrared Measurements	Range Instrumentation
Laser Applications	Space Optics
Micrography	Transportation Studies
Multispectral Sensing	Underwater Photography
Optical Communications	Underwater Research
Optical Data Reduction	X-Ray

For information on ISOE, write to International Society for Optical Engineering, P.O. Box 10, Bellingham, WA 98227.

AMERICAN SOCIETY FOR PHOTOGRAMMETRY AND REMOTE SENSING

Photogrammetry, as defined by the American Society of Photogrammetry and Remote Sensing, is the art, science, and technology of obtaining reliable information about physical objects and the environment through processes of recording, measuring, and interpreting photographic images and patterns of electromagnetic radiant energy and other phenomena.

An important application of photogrammetry has been the compilation of topographic maps and surveys, complete with contour lines, based on measurements and information obtained from aerial and space photographs.

Another application of photogrammetry is called remote sensing, in which an image is recorded by means of electronic scanning, microwaves, radar, or by thermal infrared, ultraviolet, and multispectral sensors. Remote-sensing imagery is used for the production of conventional maps, thematic maps, and resource surveys.

In addition to topographic mapping, photogrammetry is used in aerospace, agriculture, archaeology, architecture, dentistry, engineering, forestry, geology, medicine, oceanography, and urban planning in such diverse applications as highway and traffic studies, ecological studies, military science, structural analysis, and anatomy studies. Employment possibilities exist in federal, state, provincial, and local government organizations; educational institutions; and private industry.

Persons desiring to become career photogrammetrists should acquire a fundamental background in physical mathematics in addition to scientific and technical subjects. The professional photogrammetrist is usually a college graduate who develops practical knowledge through experience and continuing education. Technicians complete high school and usually attend technical colleges for additional training.

Remote sensing and photogrammetry are an integral part of many programs at colleges and universities in the United States and Canada. Course titles include Photointerpretation, Photogeology, Astrogeology, Photogrammetry, and Image Processing.

For further information on careers in photogrammetry, write to the American Society for Photogrammetry and Remote Sensing, 5410 Grosvenor Lane, Suite 210, Bethesda, MD 20814.

BIOMEDICAL PHOTOGRAPHY

One of the most exciting careers in photography today is in the field of biomedical photography. Medical schools, hospitals, research institutions, and veterinary facilities offer the biomedical photographer a great deal of diversity in job opportunities.

The scope of biomedical photography does not limit the types of photography you will do. The biomedical photographer still does nature, field, public relations, portrait, and copy photography. But in addition to these basic tasks, the photographer also photographs patients and operating room procedures, produces photomicrographs, and is involved in television production.

In order to work in this area, the biomedical photographer must have a thorough knowledge of photography as well as a basic understanding and interest in the medical and biological sciences. Training in the use of computers and computer graphics is important.

Photographs produced by biomedical photographers are used in a variety of ways. Some are used in scientific research, some are utilized in medical education, others are published in journals or brochures or displayed at scientific conferences and seminars. Obviously, the biomedical photographer has a unique opportunity to contribute both to the field of photography and to advancements in the fields of medical and biological science.

If you are interested in this branch of photography, visit a local hospital, medical school, or research institution that has photographic facilities so you can see firsthand what the job is all about.

In the past, biomedical photographers prepared for their careers through on-the-job training. Now, several schools throughout the United States offer formal programs that lead to either associate degrees or bachelor's degrees in biomedical photography. Some schools also offer master's degree-level courses in the area of biomedical communications. These courses cover such areas as communication and educational theory and broaden the scope of the photographer's production skills.

The biomedical photographic communications program at the Rochester Institute of Technology (RIT) provides a curriculum leading to a Bachelor of Science degree. The program is designed to prepare the student for a career in media production within the scientific community. Typical courses include the following:

Biomedical Photography I & II
Survey of Biomedical Photography
Color Printing

Preparation of Biomedical Visuals
Medical Terminology
Digital Photography
AV Production
Liberal Arts core courses

The biomedical photographer can be part of allied health teams in hospitals, medical and dental research centers, or in other health institutions. The Biological Photographic Association (BPA) has cooperated with RIT in development of the biomedical photography program, which can provide the educational background to qualify as a registered biological photographer (RBP), after the student enters into the profession full-time.

In addition to the formal education available in school, the Biological Photographic Association sponsors two one-week workshops in biomedical photography. The BPA also conducts a registration program for those who want to be recognized as competent in the area of biomedical photography. To become a registered biological photographer, you must undergo the BPA's three-part program, which consists of a written examination, a series of practical examinations, and an oral examination.

Lists of schools teaching biomedical photography as well as information on the registration program can be obtained by writing to the Biological Photographic Association, 109 Peachtree Street, Atlanta, Georgia 30309.

PHOTOGRAPHY IN LAW ENFORCEMENT

Law enforcement photography is a challenge—as great a challenge as the process of solving crimes. Learning all the ways photography can be used in law enforcement provides an endless source of work and study for the proficient photographer, as well as for the investigators who depend upon photography to document evidence.

An organization dedicated to bettering evidence photography both in and out of law enforcement is the Evidence Photographers International Council. EPIC developed a formal Standard for Crime Scene Photography that makes simple and orderly the approach to the law enforcer's difficulties. EPIC has stated its belief that if the standard could be adopted nationwide by all law enforcement agencies, the rate of convictions in the courts would increase dramatically.

The civil side of forensic photography supports many photographers. Their expertise varies from the simplest concept of picture-snapping to sophisticated work with excellent equipment. It seems inevitable that this group will increase, although opportunities are scarce for instruction and training.

One specialty of great interest is that of the examiner of questionable documents. Some workers seem attracted to this discipline, possibly because it demands constant effort to keep up with developments in detection methods.

EPIC is planned after the pattern of the British Qualifying Associations in that it allows serious workers to submit to an honors program. If successful, the candidate may obtain either an associateship or a fellowship in evidence photography. This citation is increasingly accepted in the courts as part of the qualifying procedures to serve as expert photographic witnesses under the rules and regulations of United States courts.

EPIC membership is open to qualified persons. Annual membership dues cover the cost of the *Journal of Evidence Photography*. The address is EPIC, 600 Main Street, Honesdale, PA 18431.

CHAPTER 8

CAREERS IN PHOTOJOURNALISM

This important aspect of photography includes work done for newspapers and magazines, wire services, and other instances where the photographer records everyday events for publication. An excellent description of a photojournalist was written by the late Arthur Rothstein in his book *Photojournalism,* published by Amphoto:

> Photojournalists are the observers of people and events who report what is happening in photographs; interpreters of facts and occurrences who write with a camera; skilled communicators whose images are transmitted visually via the printed page. Their audience consists of the readers of newspapers and magazines all over the world. Their subject is this planet and its inhabitants in all aspects, for the photographic image speaks directly to the mind and transcends the barriers of language and nationality.

Many press, television, and wire service photographers associate themselves with their own state chapter and national office of the National Press Photographers Association and subscribe to the *News Photographer* magazine, while many magazine photographers are affiliated with the American Society of Media Photographers and receive its monthly bulletin.

Another photographic specialty is photography for corporate annual reports. These printed and illustrated reports are published for the public as well as for stockholders. Competition for this work is quite high, but the prize often includes an opportunity to do subsequent publications work for corporations.

Some photojournalists find an outlet for their work in the production of slides used in slide shows and other multimedia projection programs. Such programs are shown by corporations and institutions at public gatherings, trade shows, conventions, and sales meetings. In addition to producing photographs for these productions, a knowledge of how the programs are put together, and familiarization with the mechanics and electronics involved, can be valuable.

APTITUDES NEEDED

In the fields of press, wire service, magazine, and annual report photography, there is a common denominator in terms of evaluating the person behind the camera. Academic education alone will not be enough to draw the line between the pro and the novice. He or she must be strong enough physically, mentally alert at all times, eager, and willing to go anywhere on a moment's notice and come back with pictures that tell the story, regardless of the conditions encountered. In this business, competition is keen among the top names—the picture comes first and the photographer comes in a close second. Many a camera has been smashed and many an injury inflicted upon photographers while doing their duty to get pictures of top news-breaking stories of riots, floods, strikers' picket lines, celebrities, sporting events, and wars. Even when the editor of the newspaper or the news director senses the possibility that danger is involved, the photographer often arrives on the scene without knowing all the facts and starts making pictures before encountering trouble.

Competent photographers realize that top quality and good composition have to coexist with tight deadline pressure. While the commercial photographer has to keep a top-notch business going, the photojournalist has to go one better, as far as speed and meeting deadlines are concerned. A matter of even five minutes—given today's rapid picture processing and picture transmissions via wire, radio, and satellite—could mean the difference of a "scoop" by the competitive paper, TV station, or wire service. This five-minute scoop could mean that the whole nation would first learn of the big news break because of one photographer's alertness and speed.

The mood, atmosphere, and conditions existing at the time an event occurs have to be recorded in a hurry with a 35mm camera and film or videotape by the photojournalist. In other words, he or she is a reporter with a camera. The photographer will not be able to rewrite the story, as the reporter can do. The photographer must take the attitude that "it is now or never" and make a practice of thinking this way even on routine assignments. Bill Strode, a national newspaper photographer of the year, once said, "I tackle my routine assignments as if they were assignments of national importance." Another name press photographer said, "When you tackle a new assignment in the same old way, you are beaten before you get started." A lesson to be learned in photojournalism is that in this business, you have to always be alert and use good common sense and judgment in order to come back with the picture story.

Meeting big-name people—such as movie and television stars, stars of the sports world, and politicians—and being an eyewitness to the breaking of top news stories is exciting and glamorous when reading about it, but having to go on a moment's notice to do an assignment and not know the conditions under which you will be working can become a little tiresome. Being away from your family, going into dangerous places, and being exposed to diseases and severe weather conditions are all things to take into consideration when choosing photojournalism as a career. One only has to follow the marvelous pictures in *National Geographic, Time, Newsweek,*

Sports Illustrated, the daily newspapers, and on television to see how important a medium photography is in today's communication.

KEEPING CURRENT

To become more knowledgeable about the photojournalism field, it would be well worth your time to visit the nearest daily newspaper photographic department and inquire about the dates of future workshops and photography exhibitions scheduled in your state. The most famous one is the annual NPPA Flying Short Course now scheduled to include college campuses or cities nearby. Photographic exhibitions, and many times the programs, presented by outstanding television, magazine, and press photographers are open to interested outsiders by paying the registration fee. Attending the courses keeps one up-to-date on the latest techniques and affords the opportunity to talk directly with top photographers.

Most colleges have evening photographic classes and workshops scheduled through their continuing education departments. Also, check with photo supply stores for the dates of other industry courses.

EQUIPMENT USED

As to the amount of equipment needed for coverage of photo stories and news photographs, the press and magazine photographer has a slight advantage, with some exceptions, over the television camera operator. It is surprising the amount of work that a top-notch news photographer can do with a 35mm camera, a couple of lenses, and a pocketful of 35mm film, although when going on a planned assignment, he or she may take two or three camera bodies with wide-angle, normal, and long focal length lenses, color and black-and-white film, as well as a small electronic flash. A videographer or cinematographer often is seen with a heavy tripod and a large camera. The equipment is much bulkier and heavier to carry; so is the lighting equipment. Today's portable cameras and lenses are much improved in weight, and modern videocameras are lightweight and shoulder-mounted or handheld, but there is still some extra weight and bulkiness that the movie or television person must handle.

A still photographer normally can find a privately owned studio or darkroom facilities in almost any community where he or she is doing a job to get help in film processing and making a few prints. A number of sports stadiums in colleges and universities have darkroom facilities, as well as wirephoto transmission rooms, for the photographer who must have immediate processing and transmission equipment.

On special trips with the President of the United States, or while covering high-level diplomatic conferences between world leaders, political conventions, world fairs, and the like, temporary darkrooms or permanent laboratories are made available for rush processing of films and prints. At events like the Olympics, world fairs, Democratic and Republican national conventions, and other events of national interest, the Eastman Kodak Company and Fuji will install processing equipment and furnish technical aid and assistance to help speed the processing of films and prints for all the photographers covering these events. Also, Leica, Nikon, Canon, Pentax, and other photographic equipment firms stand by with spare equipment and repair services.

NEWS SERVICE EMPLOYMENT

Anyone interested in applying for employment as a press photographer with any of the nation's newspapers or news services, will find the following sources of information helpful:

International Editor & Publisher Yearbook
    850 Third Avenue
    New York, NY 10022

General Manager
    Associated Press
    50 Rockefeller Plaza
    New York, NY 10020

ETHICAL CONSIDERATIONS

The role of the photojournalist includes fulfilling a certain measure of public trust. Readers of newspapers, magazines, and books must be able to trust that photos they see are genuine representations of the truth. The same is true of other applications of the photojournalist's work.

The National Press Photographers Association (NPPA) has developed a code of ethics to guide photographers in this area. Members are asked to subscribe to the following:

1. The practice of photojournalism, both as a science and art, is worthy of the very best thought and effort of those who enter into it as a profession.
2. Photojournalism affords an opportunity to serve the public that is equaled by few other vocations and all members of the profession should strive by example and influence to maintain high standards of ethical conduct free of mercenary considerations of any kind.
3. It is the individual responsibility of every photojournalist at all times to strive for pictures that report truthfully, honestly and objectively.
4. Business promotion in its many forms is essential, but untrue statements of any nature are not worthy of a professional photojournalist and we severely condemn any such practice.

5. It is our duty to encourage and assist all members of our profession, individually and collectively, so that the quality of photojournalism may constantly be raised to higher standards.

6. It is the duty of every photojournalist to work to preserve all freedom-of-the-press rights recognized by law and to work to protect and expand freedom-of-access to all sources of news and visual information.

7. Our standards of business dealings, ambitions and relations shall have in them a note of sympathy for our common humanity and shall always require us to take into consideration our highest duties as members of society. In every situation in our business life, in every responsibility that comes before us, our chief thought shall be to fulfill that responsibility and discharge that duty so that when each of us is finished we shall have endeavored to life the level of human ideals and achievement higher than we found it.

8. No Code of Ethics can prejudge every situation, thus common sense and good judgment are required in applying ethical principles.

CHAPTER 9

RELATED OPPORTUNITIES

The ability to use a camera competently, along with access to a supply of film and a processing lab, do not necessarily make an individual a photographer. Chances of making a decent living that covers all expenses are slim. Anybody can start a business, but keeping the business flourishing and viable for a number of years is something else. The attrition rate for small businesses of any kind is great. Business and marketing know-how are imperative in addition to having a salable skill as a photographer.

Competition also is keen among young people seeking employment as photographers. Each year, additional hundreds of graduates from photography courses are eager to begin their working life as photographers—more job-seekers than can possibly be absorbed by the business community. Obviously, the most talented and best qualified persons will fill the vacant positions.

What about those who do not find employment as photographers? The purpose of this chapter is to list the many positions and job titles other than photographer. We will describe in detail those segments of the imaging industry that offer the greatest number of opportunities. The actual camera work, while indispensable to it, is only one step in the fascinating process of imaging. Many other positions offer challenges and compensations that are equal to, and sometimes greater than, that of photographer. These include, to name just a few: technical and manufacturers' representatives, marketing specialists, public relations specialists, technical writers, equipment maintenance persons, retail salespersons, and believe it or not, buyers of photography. Art directors at advertising agencies and corporations increasingly are coming from photographic backgrounds.

SPECIALTIES AND JOB TITLES

Career opportunities related to still photography, film, and television are many and varied. Image-making and audiovisual production represent a great number of different talents and skills. This list was compiled in order to provide the student and counselor alike with most of the specialties and job titles in the world of imaging.

archivist
assistant camera operator
AV equipment technician
AV programmer
black-and-white printer
camera repairer
chief photographer
cinematographer
color printer
color production manager
colorist
darkroom supervisor
darkroom technician
director of AV communications
director of photo services
director of photography
editor of photo magazine
film archivist

forensic photographer
freelance photographer
gallery director
home economist
image analyst
image interpreter
industrial photographer
instructor
laboratory assistant
laboratory technician
manager of photographic
    equipment
manager of photographic
    services
marketing specialist in
    photography
media specialist
medical photographer

motion picture camera operator
museum curator
photo equipment technician
photo interpreter
photo lab technician
photo librarian
photofinisher
photogrammetrist
photographer
photographer's agent
photographer's assistant
photographer's representative
photographic processing and
    finishing manager
photographic technician
photographic technologist
photography director
picture editor
picture researcher
professor
public relations specialist
quality control technician
quality controller

research photographer
retail salesperson
retoucher
sales manager
senior photographer
staff photographer
still photographer
studio manager
studio receptionist
stylist
supervisor of photo electronics
supervisor of photo services
teacher
technical representative
technical writer
video producer
video technician
videocamera operator
videographer
videotape editor
web page designer
writer

PHOTOGRAPHIC PROCESSING AND FINISHING

Working as a photographic laboratory or darkroom technician—processing and finishing photographs—is a true craft that offers many opportunities for those who qualify. Some photography studios will pay as much for a qualified darkroom technician as for a photographer, and some will pay more. The ability to create a fine, finished work of art is rare, as is the person who is not anxious to burst out of the darkroom and try to become a photographer. For those who are willing to spend their working hours completing, and at times improving upon, someone else's photography, the rewards can be quite satisfying.

Professional photographic processing laboratories offer employment opportunities for qualified technicians and managers. These laboratories offer custom services of film processing and printing to professional photography studios and to corporate photographic departments.

Custom enlargement prints of color originals has become so automated and commonplace today that there is more demand for individuals who can produce quality black-and-white enlargements. There are excellent job opportunities for skilled technicians in this reemerging facet of darkroom work.

Large-scale photofinishing for the amateur market is almost exclusively color today. Photofinishing is a very competitive business, one that relies on large volumes of work coming in from route pickup and mail order business every day. The processing and printing equipment is very automated with extensive use of electronics. According to *Photo Marketing* magazine, "Photofinishing training has moved into the computer age along with the equipment that itself has become highly computerized."

The 1980s and 1990s witnessed the growth of small, one-hour minilabs in high customer traffic areas all over the country. Such labs are either independently owned or are franchise operations tied in with other minilabs. The processing equipment is compact and automated, so only several people are needed to process the color negative films, make prints, sort the orders, and wait on customers at the counter. Although the manufacturers of the automated processing equipment say that little technical skill is necessary for proper operation of the equipment, some training is imperative.

Students interested in a career in processing and finishing (on both professional/custom and volume amateur levels) should inquire at nearby processing laboratories about possible part-time summer employment. Whenever you have the opportunity to work a few weeks, or months, in any lab or studio, you should do it. There is nothing that will help you decide whether you would like to spend your life working in a specific job as actually doing that type of work for a while. It does not matter if you are just cleaning up the place, mixing chemicals, or doing some other less glamorous job. The experience itself will help you make up your mind about the future.

While the Photo Marketing Association does not endorse or recommend any particular schools for obtaining training in photofinishing, it does have literature available for individuals thinking about a career in the photofinishing industry. To obtain a copy of the brochure entitled *Photofinishing Careers,* write: Information Center, Photo Marketing Association International, 3000 Picture Place, Jackson, MI 49202.

Training at these schools would qualify graduates for employment at laboratories catering to either professionals or amateurs. Write to these schools for information and a catalog to help you determine your major interest and the overall cost of the course. Also check with schools in your region to see if they offer programs or courses in this area.

Dakota County Technical College
  1300 145th Street East
  Rosemount, MN 55068

Lansing Community College
  Photo Program Media
  Dept. 52, P.O. Box 40010
  Lansing, MI 48901

Randolph Community College
  P.O. Drawer 1009
  Asheboro, NC 27203
  (two-year program)

Rochester Institute of Technology
  Photographic Processing and Finishing Management
  One Lomb Memorial Drive
  Rochester, NY 14623
  (four-year degree program)

PHOTO RETAILING

Increased sales in the photography industry have emphasized the need for more and better qualified sales and management people. The growing sophistication of consumers and of photo products demands better educated sales and management people to meet the growing economic challenge.

A career in photo retailing can be a lucrative and rewarding step in your future—if you have an interest in photography and like to deal with the public, and you have a desire to turn that interest into a profitable future. A successful salesperson can earn the respect of the public and can earn a good financial return as well.

Outside of the major photographic manufacturers' training programs (where one must be a full-time employee to participate), there are a number of short courses and schools with curricula oriented to direct sales techniques. Photographic products and equipment selling requires specialized people to do the job well.

Traditionally, high school and junior college organizations such as the Distributive Education Clubs of America have offered opportunities for young people to learn the retail trade. These organizations are still excellent sources for trained retail personnel for the business community. An inquiry at your local camera store could possibly lead to information about a photography course in your area.

PHOTO EQUIPMENT TECHNOLOGY

A career in photo equipment technology can be profitable and rewarding. Increasingly, a knowledge of electronics, especially of microprocessors, is necessary to understand what makes photographic equipment work. A private business devoted to equipment repair and service can be especially profitable.

General service organizations employ service managers, estimators, warranty repair specialists, aerial camera service specialists, designers, and accessory installers. Photographic manufacturers need photoinstrumentation and service specialists, inspectors, estimators, warranty repair technicians, research assistants, service training managers, consumer relations specialists, and quality control technicians. Distributing and sales organizations predict a steady increase in employment for service managers, field service representatives, installation technicians, instructors, modification technicians, and customer service managers.

Industry and government opportunities are available as instrumentation specialists, modifications designers and builders, equipment maintenance technicians, test operators, and researchers and consultants. General photo equipment servicing, commercial installations, studio equipment maintenance, identification systems repair, broadcast and nonbroadcast video equipment maintenance, and school visual aids systems maintenance also offer job opportunities.

The Society of Photo-Technologists promotes technical knowledge in the field of photographic equipment repair and encourages sound operational standards and ethical business practices. For information write to:

Society of Photo-Technologists
  367 Windsor Highway
  Box 404
  New Windsor, NY 12553

A number of schools offer courses in camera repair. Today's complex, electronic cameras mean the student must study about both mechanical and electronic workings of cameras. Repair technicians must be able to quickly diagnose problems and make repairs. If you are interested, check with technical schools in your area to see if courses in camera repair are offered or if other related courses might provide some background. Also check with repair shops to see if you can learn on the job.

PHOTOGRAPHY AS ART

Through the years, much has been said and written about the relationship of photography to other art media. The acceptance of photographic exhibits in art museums has made tremendous advancement in recent years in spite of reluctance by some museum officials to devote space and publicity to photography.

A close relationship between art and photography can be traced back to the experiments of Thomas Wedgwood in 1802, when he was inspired by paintings to make his camera exposures. Even Sir Humphry Davy's production of silhouettes could be considered a contribution to the beginning of artistic composition as it is applied to photography.

One of the earliest photographs reproduced strictly for its picturesque quality was "The Open Door," which William Henry Fox Talbot used in *The Pencil of Nature* in 1844. Another early contribution to the use of photography as an illustration medium was when "The Lord's Prayer" was illustrated with a series of ten daguerreotypes by J. J. E. Mayall in 1845. Peter Henry Emerson, one of the most important nineteenth-century photographers, produced an edition of 200 of his *Life and Landscape of the Norfolk Broads.* In 1973, one of these sets sold for $2,500; three years later the reported price was close to $22,000.

More recent photographers whose work contributed much to the elevation of photography as an art were Edward Weston, Walker Evans, Wynn Bullock, Minor White, Edward Steichen, and Paul Strand. A print by Ansel Adams that sold for $150 in 1970 would bring many thousands of dollars today. A leading New York photo gallery sells prints by contemporary photographers for $150 to $750. Gallery commissions range from 40 to 60 percent, depending upon arrangements agreed upon between the gallery and the photographer.

In the 1970s and 1980s, prices of photographic prints sold at art galleries began to rise. At the same time, many more art galleries started to handle photographs. Even top New York City galleries, such as Christie's and Sotheby's, regularly conduct photo auctions today. Five-figure amounts for a recognized photographer's work are not uncommon. Rare photographs, with strong prices, have become a routine item at these prestigious galleries. Today, there seems to be a continuing healthy demand for quality photography for display, or as an investment for appreciation in value.

With the development of dye transfer and other direct color techniques, color photographic portraiture is hanging in banks, public buildings, homes, museums, meeting rooms, and the many other places where oil portraits once predominated. Many fine portrait studios throughout the country are selling large color photographs. Previously, portrait artists working in oil had monopolized this lucrative business.

Photographs are increasingly used as decoration in business offices, manufacturing plants, hospitals, restaurants, and other public places. Several professional processing laboratories offer advice and aid in preparing photographs for decorative purposes.

FEDERAL GOVERNMENT

The majority of the photographers working in the federal government are in the U.S. Air Force, Army, and Navy, as well as in the Departments of Justice, Transportation, Energy, Environmental Protection, Agriculture, Health and Human Services, and Veterans Affairs, and in the National Aeronautics and Space Administration.

Optional photographic fields classified by the U.S. Civil Service Commission are: aerial, laboratory, medical, motion picture, scientific and technical, still, television, underwater, and general.

General experience qualifications for federal photographer classifications include experience in (1) operating such cameras and related equipment such as still cameras, copy cameras, and 16mm motion picture cameras; (2) carrying out common developing and printing processes and related techniques; or a combination of both (1) and (2). This general experience must demonstrate increasing ability to exercise artistic ability in selecting, arranging, and lighting the subject, or in processing, printing, enlarging, and retouching prints, or in both areas. Advanced photographic training in residence at a technical trade school beyond the high school level or at a recognized college or university can better qualify you for specialized fields, provided that such training is directly related to the optional field for which application is made.

Applicants are invited to mention any awards, prizes, or commendations received for their photographic work and any publication or exhibition of their photographic work. Samples of photographs may be required to establish eligibility for some positions, but only when specifically requested.

Information and application forms for the above Civil Service positions are available at all post offices.

The Armed Forces

One option is going to one of the military photography schools and utilizing military time to build a good foundation for a lifetime photography career. Some leading photographers got their start in the military service. There is no end to the number of civilian employees working in commercial, industrial, portraiture, photojournalism, and other related fields who received their first photographic training in one of the branches of the military.

The advantage of being able to travel, meet people of other countries, and see firsthand how they live, while gaining experience with the large variety of cameras and processing equipment the military provides, is quite a bargain and should not be overlooked. The major disadvantage, of course, is the risk of being sent into combat or other hazardous situations if a war or military conflict erupts. Military service involves a serious commitment that should not be taken lightly.

A phone call or visit to the recruiting office of your preferred branch of service will give answers to specific questions. Each of the recruiting offices is listed under "U.S. Government" in the telephone directory of large cities and most county seats. School counselors also are supplied with much military material.

The chances of being assigned to photography in the armed forces would depend on the extent of one's photography education and experience, aptitude tests and interviews, physical examination, changes in photography as a communication medium, and the current demand for photographic personnel.

Military pay and rank advances are governed by Acts of Congress and the Defense Department's recommendation. There are stipulations giving hazardous and overseas duty higher rates of pay. Insurance, education, and veteran's benefits, plus other advantages such as retirement at a younger age than is possible for most persons in business, should not be overlooked when thinking of a possible career in military photography.

Duty in military photography could be any place in the world, on ships at sea, at the battlefront, on a submarine exploration trip under the North Pole, on an expedition to the Antarctic, on flights into outer space, in the deserts of the Middle East, or on some remote island.

FILM AND TELEVISION

The motion picture and television fields can provide an interesting and fulfilling career. It takes a great variety of skills to produce a feature film or a major television program. Competition for technical and professional positions is high, especially in Hollywood and New York. Talents range from camera operators to lighting technicians, from animators to film processors and videotape editors.

The glamour of Hollywood and New York will always attract more talent than can possibly be employed. And, while we would never presume to discourage a genuine desire to pursue a career in the "big time," you might instead consider a career in corporate or nonbroadcast film and television production.

OPPORTUNITIES FOR PEOPLE WITH DISABILITIES

Several areas of photography offer employment opportunities for people with disabilities. Housebound and wheelchair-bound persons who are artistic and who have good eyesight and fair agility with the hands can be employed by photography studios, or they can be self-employed as artists. These artists are negative retouchers for portrait photographers, oil colorists and painters for portrait photographers, or airbrush artists for portrait and commercial studios. The rudiments of portrait negative retouching and oil coloring can be learned in courses.

A career in photo equipment technology also can be profitable and rewarding to many disabled persons. Again, those with good eyesight and ability with the hands can be excellent candidates for equipment maintenance and repair.

Visually impaired workers can work in photofinishing. As in the past, the blind and near-blind are being trained on photographic equipment. Through the expansion of the photo lab facilities at the Center for the Visually Impaired in Denver, greater numbers of the visually impaired have had the opportunity for complete training afforded to only a few in the past. The program was developed with the cooperation of the Eastman Kodak Company, the Center for the Visually Impaired, the National Industries for the Blind, and the Photo Marketing Association.

The National Technical Institute for the Deaf in Rochester, NY, was created to provide deaf students with the technological training that will lead to meaningful employment in business, industry, government, and education. Public Law 89-36 authorized the establishment of NTID, and Rochester Institute of Technology was chosen as the sponsoring institution. Classes have been held there since 1968. The fact that NTID is located on a regular college campus is seen as an important factor in the development of personal, social, and communication competence of deaf students.

Educational opportunities are available for deaf students on both the community and senior college levels. The NTID Division of Technical Education offers deaf students certificate, diploma, and associate degree programs in the sciences, technologies, and applied arts. The division has seven departments, including Visual Communications Technologies, which offers a Certificate in Applied Photography, a Diploma in Applied Photography, and an Associate in Applied Science in Applied Photography. Through the various colleges of RIT, qualified NTID students are able to pursue baccalaureate degree programs. For further information contact:

Coordinator of Vocational Rehabilitation Affairs
  NTID, Rochester Institute of Technology
  One Lomb Memorial Drive
  Rochester, NY 14623

OPPORTUNITIES IN TEACHING

In the past, the teaching of photography was frequently a part-time activity of a professional photographer, who either needed additional income or enjoyed contact with students through the sharing of his or her photographic knowledge. Increasingly, however, teaching became professionalized, until today it is a specific discipline of its own. The emphasis is thus shifting from merely accumulating photographic skills and experiences to a working knowledge of the complex interpersonal behavior we know as teaching. In today's highly competitive job market, it is seldom enough to have only the basic skills and accomplishments of a good photographer—the aspiring teacher must also know how to communicate that information in a way that facilitates the growth of his or her students.

There is an increasingly wide variety of ways in which photography is being taught and utilized in contemporary school systems. These ways may be classed as follows:

Vocational. This is usually a two-year program, offered in many community or technical colleges or in trade or vocational schools. Colleges may offer a two-year associate degree or a one-year certificate. Vocational schools will more likely offer some type of certificate that takes a year or less to complete. Typically these programs emphasize the technical aspects of photography, with the purpose of giving the student sufficient job-entry skills to begin making his or her living in the field of commercial, industrial, medical, or portrait photography.

Fine Arts. These programs are generally in either art schools or four-year colleges or universities. The curriculum focuses on the use of photography as an expressive medium, much as drawing, painting, sculpture, dance, or music. In a purely fine arts–oriented program, there is no intent of preparing the student to enter the world of commercial photography, as the primary emphasis is on esthetics, self-expression, history of the medium, and the relationship of photography to other expressive media.

Multipurpose. Some college, university, and art school programs are large enough to offer a two-track curriculum, with one track leading into commercial applications of photography, while the other track leads in a fine arts direction. Such a program requires a faculty with a very broad background of training and professional experience, which is not frequently found in any one school.

Liberal Arts. This is not usually a full major program, but rather a series of courses that offer the student a photographic experience without attempting to prepare him or her for a career in photography.

Specialty Programs. Many schools at both the secondary and postsecondary level have specialty courses in photography designed to fill needs in specific professional areas, such as journalism, science, and medicine. These programs, of course, require faculties with very specialized and often extensive training and experience in the specific discipline.

Ancillary Programs. There is a growing awareness on the part of many professional disciplines—from psychotherapy to anthropology—of the necessity of acquiring a knowledge of photography. These courses or programs, therefore, are designed for the individual who already has a professional background, but who wants to add photographic skills. The teacher in such a program generally needs at least a working knowledge not only of photography, but also of the related profession.

Academic Requirements

Each type or level of school system has its own academic requirements that a teacher must complete to be eligible for employment in the system. There are exceptions to these, but following are the general requirements for each type of system:

Elementary and Secondary Schools. These require an undergraduate degree plus state certification to teach at the appropriate level. Recently, many secondary schools are requiring a master's degree in the area of specialization, if the teacher is to be in charge of a full program.

Community/Technical Colleges. These schools often require the master's degree in the area of specialization, and many systems also require state certification. This is currently the most expansive area of photographic education, both in terms of programs and salaries.

Four-Year Colleges and Universities. There is often a certain amount of flexibility in the requirements for short-term employment at the college level, but tenure usually requires that the faculty member have the terminal degree in his or her area of specialization. In the case of photography, this is the Master of Fine Arts degree (M.F.A.). At one time, this could be completed after the teacher was hired, but with the current large crop of M.F.A. graduates, this practice is no longer as common. Additionally, the prospective teacher must have demonstrated his or her photographic ability, usually in terms of exhibitions and/or publications.

Vocational Schools. The applied nature of these programs requires that the teacher have professional and commercial experience. Many schools often require that their faculty continue to be active commercially, to keep abreast of new developments and practices. Additionally, depending upon the accrediting agency with which the school is affiliated, the faculty also may need an academic degree.

Private Schools. The requirements in private schools at all levels are generally more flexible than those in public or state schools, but this also varies with the requirements imposed by the accrediting body with which the school is affiliated.

Workshops and Alternative Schools. These organizations have the most flexibility of all, with hiring usually based on demonstrated ability and little concern for academic background. This, too, varies with the school or workshop's accreditation. Those institutions that give academic credit to students and participants must meet the same standards as do other credit-awarding institutions.

Personal Qualities

While few individuals possess all the attributes of the "ideal teacher," there are some characteristics that would seem essential for anyone who wishes to teach photography as a career.

The photography teacher—like any other classroom teacher—needs strong group leadership and classroom management skills to efficiently organize her or his classes in order to carry out the class objectives and goals.

The ideal photography teacher would be a combination carpenter/plumber/electrician/mechanic. With tight school budgets at all levels, the teacher who can work on the myriad problems that occur in even the best photo facilities will be in a much better position to keep a program running smoothly. The photography teacher also must be a budget-maker in most programs, often responsible for large sums spent on supplies and equipment.

The teacher who is also an artist or commercial photographer must learn to work with the inherent conflict of trying to maintain both roles at a professional level of competence. One of the major problems reported by such teachers is the split among their available time, energy, and resources.

Above all, the aspiring teacher must want to work with *people.* Despite the emphasis in the media on photographic techniques and equipment, photography is done by human beings. Without a genuine respect for the individual student, no meaningful educational dialogue can occur.

Salaries for teaching photography are generally comparable with other arts or professional skills. There is usually no additional compensation for the added responsibilities of teaching a laboratory subject. In some secondary schools, however, there may be additional money for directing a photo club after normal school hours, or advising the student newspaper. Additional outside income may come from judging exhibitions, consulting with other schools, or holding workshops.

Regardless of any other differences of opinion, most photography teachers will agree that theirs is a job that requires long hours—there is always something more that the conscientious teacher can do. From this standpoint, the photographers who look to a career in teaching to give themselves time to do their own work are likely to be sadly disillusioned. Except for the possibility of usually unpaid summer vacation, the teaching of photography is a full-time job. However, for the man or woman who deeply enjoys working with both photography and people, the teaching of photography can be an eminently satisfying career.

Society for Photographic Education

Many schools now offer courses that result in either Ph.D. or Ed.D. degrees in motion picture, still, or graphic arts photography. Offering such courses are: Boston University, Princeton University, Northwestern University, New York University, University of Chicago, University of New Mexico, University of Oregon, University of Texas at Austin, and University of Southern California. Studying with the goal of becoming a professor of photography may be a wise decision.

The Society for Photographic Education (SPE), an organization of about 1,500 teachers of photography on both the secondary and college level, was organized to promote high standards of photographic education, to assist members on matters relating to academic freedom, and to increase public awareness of the art of photography.

Most active members are photography instructors with degrees and are full-time employees of leading educational institutions in the United States. Photographic classes taught by SPE members are, in most cases, part of art department curricula and limited to art majors. The classes are normally full, with waiting lists of students hoping to get into the classes the next school term. The curricula are basic and art-related, and they emphasize creativity.

In recent years there has been an increased awareness among SPE members, and among almost all photography studio owners and their professional associations, of the importance of advanced and professional-directed training for preparing graduates for both instructional and professional photography careers. One result has been the increasing number of Director of Education titles appearing on staff listings of photographic manufacturers and professional photography associations

CHAPTER 10

CONTINUING EDUCATION AND PROFESSIONAL DEVELOPMENT

The methods, supplies, equipment, and techniques used in photography are constantly changing. To keep current and up-to-date, each photographer and lab technician should seriously consider taking some advanced studies or refresher courses. Today there is an abundance of seminars, workshops, conferences, conventions, and short courses that deal with just about all photographic subjects. Sponsors include societies and associations, magazines, photographic manufacturers and distributors, colleges and universities, and private and public institutions. Since these groups are vitally concerned with the improvement and progress of the profession of photography, they tend to keep the costs of such instruction to a minimum, since they help the overall cause of photography.

Once you seriously decide to become involved with some aspect of photography, there are many opportunities and ways you can enhance your knowledge in a minimum of time.

A wide range of periodicals offer a continuous flow of technical, esthetic, and business information on all forms of imaging. These magazines and journals constitute an essential source of information and provide an invaluable service to the industry.

A relatively recent development in the continuing education of those in still photography, film, and video is training programs via audiovisual media. These lessons are on slides and cassette tapes, motion pictures, videotapes, and video discs and computer software. Topics range from still photography to video. Many subjects are presented at either the beginning or advanced level of experience.

Several nonprofit institutions contribute to the photographer's continuing education. Here are two outstanding examples:

The International Center of Photography, 1130 Fifth Avenue, New York, NY 10028, (with a second location at 1133 Avenue of the Americas in New York) is both a photography museum and a center for photographic studies and activities. Lectures, workshops, and open forums are held year-round to enable photographers to share their theories, techniques, and experiences and to discuss the development of new techniques. The center offers an internship program.

The International Museum of Photography at George Eastman House, 900 East Avenue, Rochester, NY 14607, is the largest and most important museum of photography in the world. GEH houses outstanding collections of photographs, motion picture films, and photographic equipment. The museum sponsors on-site and traveling exhibitions of historical significance and contemporary trends. George Eastman House offers a limited number of museum internships. Conferences and seminars are held throughout the year on all aspects of photography. A journal, *Image,* is published for associate members and libraries.

All associations and societies related to photography offer some form of continuing education. The annual conventions of these groups offer presentations of technical papers, panel discussions, and sessions on specialized areas. Those who attend these meetings can benefit greatly through exchange of information.

We strongly urge you to get involved, early in your career, with the association or society in your area of interest. Write to the group or groups that represent your specialty; ask for information on services offered. Inquire about student memberships and student chapters. You must be prepared to give of your time and talent to the group to which you belong. You will be repaid many times over for your efforts.

SHORT COURSES AND WORKSHOPS

Schools and colleges that offer photography programs sometimes sponsor short courses for practicing photographers or those who aspire to become professionals. In addition, companies that manufacture or sell products related to photography sometimes offer short courses, seminars, or workshops. Most firms charge "at cost" fees for attendance.

For example, manufacturers and distributors of photofinishing processing equipment conduct seminars and workshops for people who own and work with their equipment. In addition, many distributors of video and audiovisual production equipment offer hands-on experience with their products. For further information, contact the dealer or distributor nearest you.

Typical short course or workshop topics include:

Advanced Slide Preparation
Advanced Audiovisual Techniques
Use of View Cameras
Holographic Photography
Infrared and Ultraviolet Photography
Stereo Photography
Alternative Processes
Large Format Photography
The Art of Composition
Digital Color Printing

Creative Darkroom Techniques
Handcoloring Photographs
Nature Photography
Newspaper Photojournalism
Photographing Families
Architectural Photography

In recent decades, the number of several-day to week-long workshops on various photographic subjects has mushroomed dramatically. Most offer courses structured for both beginning and advanced photographers. Conducted by photo manufacturers, magazines, schools, and professional photographers, workshops are offered in locales all over the United States and Canada. Some even involve travel to foreign countries. Costs range from $100 and up, but few include meals and/or lodging. Most are offered during summer months so that individuals who attend can combine photography instruction with their vacation. Most workshops combine lectures with practical hands-on instruction for excellent learning conditions. Intense learning experiences are provided by close teacher-student rapport.

For a number of years, Kodak and Nikon have cosponsored a tuition-free, photojournalism-oriented workshop held in the fall. Called the Eddie Adams Workshop, it is open to photography students and professionals with less than two years of experience. The faculty consists of more than fifty top picture journalism professionals. Submitted applicant portfolios accompanied by letters of recommendation are reviewed, and ninety-nine talented young photographers are selected to attend. Participants pay only for transportation and room and board. In the spring, applications are distributed through newspapers, universities and colleges, and military bases and to student members of the National Press Photographers Association. If photojournalism is among your interests, you should investigate applying for this workshop.

There is a Young Photographers Workshop that provides two-week-long summer programs designed for young persons interested in black-and-white photography. The sessions cover camera basics, film, the darkroom, printmaking, and development of an individual photographic vision. Each participant develops a portfolio. For further information contact:

Maine Photography Workshops
  Attention: Young Photographers Workshop
  P.O. Box 200
  Rockport, Maine 04856

Photography Workshops

Listed here are a few of the more established workshops:

Ampro Photo Workshops
  636 East Broadway
  Vancouver, BC V5T 1X6
  Canada

Anchell Photography Workshops
  P.O. Box 277
  Crestone, CO 81131

California Natural Wonders Photography Workshops
  P.O. Box 457
  La Canada, CA 91012

Canadian Mountain Holidays Photography Workshop
  Box 1660
  Banff, AL T0L 0G0
  Canada

Cape Cod Photo Workshops
  P.O. Box 1619
  North Eastham, MA 02651

Cory Photography Workshops
  P.O. Box 42
  Signal Mountain, TN 37377

Creative Photographic Arts Center of Maine Workshops
  P.O. Box 921
  Lewiston, ME 04243–0921

Flying Short Courses
  National Press Photographers Association
  3200 Croasdaile Drive, Suite 306
  Durham, NC 27705

Great American Photography Weekend
  160 Whirlaway Trail
  Corbin, KY 40701

Great Lakes Institute of Photography
  19276 Eureka
  Southgate, MI 48195

Investigative Photography Workshops
  Federal Law Enforcement Training Center
  P.O. Box 1409
  Evanston, IL 60204

Joe Englander Photography Workshops and Tours
  P.O. Box 1261
  Manchaca, TX 78652

John Sexton Photography Workshops
  291 Los Agrinemsono
  Carmel Valley, CA 93924

Maria Zorn Nature Photography Workshops
  37 Bond Street South
  Dundas, ON L9H 3H2
  Canada

Santa Fe Workshops
  P.O. Box 9916
  Santa Fe, NM 87504

Southampton College Master Photography Workshops
  239 Montauk Highway
  Southampton, NY 11968–4198

Vermont Photography Workshop
  RR 1, Box 234
  Camp Arden Road
  Brattleboro, VT 05301

Vision Quest Photography Workshops
  2370 Herndon Avenue
  St. Paul, MN 55108

Western Academy of Photography
  755A Queens Avenue
  Victoria, BC V8T 1M2
  Canada

Youth Outlook Photography Workshop
  450 Mission Street
  San Francisco, CA 94105

PERIODICALS

Advertising Age
220 East Forty-second
Street
New York, NY 10017

American Cinematographer
1782 North Orange Drive
Los Angeles, CA 90028

American Photo
1633 Broadway
New York, NY 10019

Aperture
c/o Aperture Foundation,
Inc.
20 East Twenty-third Street
New York, NY 10010

Computer Pictures
c/o Montage Publishing, Inc.
701 Winchester Avenue
White Plains, NY 10604

*Darkroom & Creative Camera
Techniques*
7800 Merrimac Avenue
Niles, IL 60714

Electronic Photography News
10915 Bonita Beach Road
Bonita Springs, FL 33923

FotoFlash
23 Latham Avenue
Scarborough, ON M1H 1Y3
Canada

Industrial Photography
PTN Publishing Company
445 Broad Hollow Road
Melville, NY 11747

*Journal of Imaging Science
and Technology*
SIST
7003 Kilworth Lane
Springfield, VA 22151

Minilab Developments
  c/o International MiniLab
    Association
  2627 Grimsley Street
  Greensboro, NC 27403

News Photographer
  c/o NPPA
  3200 Croasdaile Drive
  Suite 306
  Durham, NC 27705

Outdoor Photographer
  12121 Wilshire Boulevard
  Los Angeles, CA 90025

*Outdoor and Travel
    Photography*
  1115 Broadway, 8th Floor
  New York, NY 10010

*Petersen's PhotoGraphic
    Magazine*
  6420 Wilshire Boulevard
  Los Angeles, CA 90048

Photo Digest
  850 Boulevard Pierre
    Betrand
  Vanier, PQ G1M 3K8
  Canada

Photo District News
  1515 Broadway
  New York, NY 10036

Photo Lab Management
  P.O. Box 1700
  1312 Lincoln Boulevard
  Santa Monica, CA 90406

Photo Life
  130 Spy Court
  Markham, ON L3R 5H6
  Canada

Photo Marketing
  3000 Picture Place
  Jackson, MI 49201

Photographer's Forum
  511 Olive Street
  Santa Barbara, CA 93101

Photographic Trade News
  445 Broad Hollow Road
  Melville, NY 11747

PhotoPro
  5211 South Washington
    Avenue
  Titusville, FL 32780

Popular Photography
  1633 Broadway
  New York, NY 10019

The Professional Photographer
  c/o PPofA
  57 Forsyth Street
  Atlanta, GA 30303

PSA Journal
   3000 United Founders
      Boulevard
   Suite 103
   Oklahoma City, OK 73112

The Rangefinder
   1312 Lincoln Boulevard
   Santa Monica, CA 90401

Shutterbug
   5211 South Washington
      Avenue
   Titusville, FL 32780

Studio Light
   Professional Photography
      Division
   Eastman Kodak Company
   343 State Street
   Rochester, NY 14650

Studio Photography
   c/o PTN Publishing Co.
   445 Broad Hollow Road
   Melville, NY 11747

*Today's Photographer
   Magazine*
   P.O. Box 777
   Lewisville, NC 27023-0777

Video Technology Newsletter
   1201 Seven Locho Road
   Potomac, MD 20854

Video Trade News
   Box 597
   Ridgefield, CT 06877

Videomaker
   Box 4591
   Chico, CA 95927

View Camera
   2774 Harkness Street
   Sacramento, CA 95818

The Wedding Photographer
   1312 Lincoln Boulevard
   Santa Monica, CA 90406

Wildlife Photography
   P.O. Box 224
   Greenville, PA 16125

ASSOCIATIONS AND SOCIETIES

A list of selected photography associations and societies, with addresses to which you may write for information, is given below.

Advertising Photographers of
New York
27 West Twentieth Street
New York, NY 10011

American Photographic
Artisan's Guild
P.O. Box 699
Fort Clinton, OH 43452

American Society of Media
Photographers (ASMP)
14 Washington Road
Suite 502
Princeton Junction, NJ
08550

American Society of
Photogrammetry
5410 Grosvenor Lane
Bethesda, MD 20814

American Society of
Photographers (ASP)
P.O. Box 3191
Spartanburg, SC 29304

American Society of Picture
Professionals
Box 5283, Grand Central
Station
New York, NY 10163

Association for Educational
Communications &
Technology (AECT)
1025 Vermont Avenue
Washington, DC 20005

Association for Information
and Image Management
1100 Wayne Avenue
Silver Spring, MD 20910

Association for Multi-Image
(AMI)
1006 North Dale Mabry
Highway
Tampa, FL 33618

Association of Professional
Color Laboratories
(APCL)
3000 Picture Place
Jackson, MI 49201

Biological Photographic
Association (BPA)
1819 Peachtree Road NE
Atlanta, GA 30309

Canadian Association of
Journalists
St. Patrick's Building,
Carleton University
1125 Colonel By Drive
Ottawa, ON K15 5B6
Canada

Canadian Association of
Photographers and
Illustrators in
Communications
100 Broadway Avenue,
Suite 322
Toronto, ON M4M 2E8
Canada

Evidence Photographers
International Council
(EPIC)
600 Main Street
Honesdale, PA 18431

International Association of
Panoramic Photographers
P.O. Box 2816
Boca Raton, FL 33427–2816

International Freelance
Photographers
Organization
P.O. Box 777
Lewiston, NC 27023

International Fire
Photographers
Association
P.O. Box 8337
Rolling Meadows, IL 60008

International Minilab
Association
2627 Grimsley Street
Greensboro, NC 27403

International Photographic
Historical Organization
P.O. Box 16074
San Francisco, CA 94116

International Society for
Optical Engineering
P.O. Box 10
Bellingham, WA 98227

National Association of
    Government
    Communicators
669 South Washington Street
Alexandria, VA 22314

National Association for
    Photographic Art
3158 Hopedale Avenue
Clearbrook, BC V2T 2G7
Canada

National Association of
    Photographic
    Manufacturers (NAPM)
550 Mamaroneck Avenue
Harrison, NY 10528

National Freelance
    Photographers
    Association
P.O. Box 406
Solebury, PA 18963

National Photographic
    Instructors Association
1255 Hill Drive
Engle Rock, CA 90041

National Press Photographers
    Association, Inc. (NPPA)
3200 Croasdaile Drive,
    Suite 306
Durham, NC 27705

NAVA, The International
    Communications
    Industries Association
3150 Spring Street
Fairfax, VA 22031

North American Nature
    Photography Association
10200 West Forty-fourth
    Avenue
Wheat Ridge, CO 80033

Optical Society of America
    (OSA)
2010 Massachusetts Avenue
    NW
Washington, DC 20036

Photo Marketing Association
    International (PMAI)
3000 Picture Place
Jackson, MI 49201

Photographic Manufacturers
    & Distributors
    Association, Inc. (PMDA)
1120 Avenue of the
    Americas
New York, NY 10036

Photographic Society of
America, Inc. (PSA)
3000 United Founders
Boulevard
Suite 103
Oklahoma City, OK 73112

Professional Film and Video
Equipment Association
P.O. Box 9436
Silver Spring, MD 20916

Professional Photographers of
America, Inc.
57 Forsyth Street NW
Atlanta, GA 30303

Professional Photographers of
Canada, Inc.
1215 Penticton Avenue
Penticton, BC V2A 2N3
Canada

Professional Photographers of
Ontario
2833 Donnelly Drive, RR #4
Kemptville, ON K0G 1J0
Canada

Professional School
Photographers of America
1000 Picture Place
Jackson, MI 49201

Professional Women
Photographers
c/o Photographics Unlimited
17 West Seventeenth Street
#14
New York, NY 10011

Society for Imaging Science
and Technology
7003 Kilworth Lane
Springfield, VA 22151

Society of Motion Picture &
Television Engineers
(SMPTE)
595 West Hartsdale Avenue
White Plains, NY 10607

Society of Photo Finishing
Engineers (SPFE)
3000 Picture Place
Jackson, MI 49201

Society for Photographic
Education (SPE)
P.O. Box 222116
Dallas, TX 75222

Society of Photo-
Technologists (SPT)
367 Windsor Highway
New Windsor, NY 12553

Society of Teachers in
    Education of Professional
    Photography
371 Greenport Drive
West Carrolton, OH 45449

University Photographers
    Association of America
c/o News Services
Western Michigan
    University
Kalamazoo, MI 49008

Wedding Photographers
    International
P.O. Box 1703
Santa Monica, CA 90406

White House News
    Photographers
    Association
7119 Ben Franklin Station
Washington, DC 20044

SCHOOLS

The following is a partial list of the more than 1,000 schools offering certificates, diplomas, and degrees with a major emphasis in photography or related areas.

CERTIFICATES AND DIPLOMAS

Daytona Beach Community
College
P.O. Box 2811
Daytona Beach, FL 32120

Fanshawe College of Applied
Arts and Technology
1460 Oxford Street
London, ON N5W 5H1
Canada

Hallmark Institute of
Photography
P.O. Box 308
Turner Falls, MA 01376

The Maine Photographic
Workshops
Rockport, ME 04856

New England School of
Photography
537 Commonwealth Avenue
Boston, MA 02215

New York Institute of
Photography
211 East Forty-third Street
New York, NY 10017

Ohio Institute of Photography
and Technology
2029 Edgefield Road
Dayton, OH 45439

A.A. OR A.S. DEGREES

Academy of Art College
  79 New Montgomery
  San Francisco, CA 94108

Ampro Photography School
  636 East Broadway
  Vancouver, BC V5T 1X6
  Canada

Antonelli College
  124 East Seventh Street
  Cincinnati, OH 45202

Antonelli Institute
  2910 Jolly Road
  Plymouth Meeting, PA
  19462

A1 Business and Technical
  College
  13–14 Dr. Rufo Street
  Caguas, PR 00726

Art Institute of Fort Lauderdale
  1799 Southeast Seventeenth
  Street
  Fort Lauderdale, FL 33316

Art Institute of Houston
  1900 Yorktown
  Houston, TX 77056

Art Institute of Philadelphia
  1622 Chestnut Street
  Philadelphia, PA 19103

The Art Institute of Pittsburgh
  526 Penn Avenue
  Pittsburgh, PA 15222

The Art Institute of Seattle
  2323 Elliott Avenue
  Seattle, WA 98121

Ball State University
  Muncie, IN 47306

Brigham Young University
  Provo, UT 84602

Brooks Institute
  801 Alston Road
  Santa Barbara, CA 93108

Chowan College
  Jones Drive
  Murfreesboro, NC 27855

Colorado Institute of Art
  200 East Ninth Avenue
  Denver, CO 80203

Daytona Beach Community
  College
  P.O. Box 2811
  Daytona Beach, FL 32120

DeAnza College
  21250 Stevens Creek
  Boulevard
  Cupertino, CA 95014

Ferris State College
901 South State
Big Rapids, MI 49307

Hallmark Institute of
Photography
P.O. Box 308
Turner Falls, MA 01376

Hawkeye Community College
Box 8015
Waterloo, IA 50704

Institute Fontecha
De Tierra Station
San Juan, PR 00906

Kilgore College
1100 Broadway
Kilgore, TX 75662

Lansing Community College
419 North Capitol Avenue
Lansing, MI 48901

Louisiana Art Institute
7380 Exchange Place
Baton Rouge, LA 70806

Milwaukee Area Technical
College
700 West State Street
Milwaukee, WI 53223

New England School of
Photography
357 Commonwealth Avenue
Boston, MA 02215

Paler College of Art
20 Gorham Avenue
Hamden, CT 06517

Phoenix College
1202 West Thomas Road
Phoenix, AZ 85035

Rochester Institute of
Technology
Lomb Memorial Drive
Rochester, NY 14623

School of Communication Arts
2526 Twenty-seventh
Avenue South
Minneapolis, MN 55406

SUTECH School of
Vocational Technical
Training
34277 East Olympic
Boulevard
Los Angeles, CA 90023

University of Bridgeport
Bridgeport, CT 06601

Western Academy of
Photography
755A Queens Avenue
Victoria, BC V8T 1M2
Canada

B.A. OR B.S. DEGREES

Arizona State University
  Tempe, AZ 85287

Ball State University
  Muncie, IN 47306

Boston University
  Boston, MA 02215

Brigham Young University
  Provo, UT 84602

Brooks Institute
  Santa Barbara, CA 93108

California State University,
  Fullerton
  Fullerton, CA 92834

Florida State University
  Tallahassee, FL 32306

Illinois Institute of Technology
  Chicago, IL 60616

Kent State University
  Kent, OH 44242

Montana State University
  Bozeman, MT 59717

Northern Michigan University
  Marquette, MI 49855

Oregon State University
  Corvallis, OR 97331

Pennsylvania State University
  University Park, PA 16802

Rochester Institute of
  Technology
  Rochester, NY 14623

Southern Illinois University
  Carbondale, IL 62901

The Richard Stockton College
  of New Jersey
  Pomona, NJ 08240

University of Bridgeport
  Bridgeport, CT 06602

University of Maryland,
  Baltimore County
  Baltimore, MD 21250

University of Minnesota
  Minneapolis, MN 55435

University of Missouri
  Columbia, MO 65211

University of Wisconsin-
  Platteville
  Platteville, WI 53818

B.F.A. AND OTHER BACHELOR'S DEGREES

Arizona State University
Tempe, AZ 85287

Brigham Young University
Provo, UT 84601

California College of Arts and
Crafts
San Francisco, CA 94107

Central Michigan University
Mount Pleasant, MI 48859

Colorado State University
Ft. Collins, CO 80523

Florida State University
Tallahassee, FL 32306

Indiana State University
Terre Haute, IN 47809

Louisiana Tech University
Ruston, LA 71272

Memphis College of Art
Memphis, TN 38104

Rhode Island School of Design
Providence, RI 02903

Rochester Institute of
Technology
Rochester, NY 14623

University of Bridgeport
Bridgeport, CT 06601

University of Dayton
Dayton, OH 45469

University of Oregon
Eugene, OR 97403

University of Rhode Island
Kingston, RI 02881

University of Saskatchewan,
Saskatoon
Saskatoon, Saskatchewan
S7N 0W0
Canada

University of Texas, Austin
Austin, TX 78712

University of Wisconsin,
Superior
Superior, WI 54880

M.A. OR M.S. DEGREES

Boston University
Boston, MA 02215

Brooks Institute
Santa Barbara, CA 93108

Northern Michigan University
Marquette, MI 49855

Southern Illinois University
Carbondale, IL 62901

Syracuse University
Syracuse, NY 13244

Texas Woman's University
Denton, TX 76204

University of Southern
California
Los Angeles, CA
90089-0292

University of Wisconsin,
Superior
Superior, WI 54880

M.F.A. AND OTHER MASTER'S DEGREES

Brooks Institute
Santa Barbara, CA 93108

Illinois Institute of Technology
Chicago, IL 60616

Louisiana Tech University
Ruston, LA 71272

Ohio University, Athens
Athens, OH 45701

Rochester Institute of
Technology
Rochester, NY 14623

Southern Illinois University
Carbondale, IL 62901

University of Minnesota
Minneapolis, MN 55435

University of Southern
California
Los Angeles, CA 90089

PH.D. OR ED.D. DEGREES

Boston University
Boston, MA 02215

New York University
New York, NY 10012

Northwestern University
Evanston, IL 60208

Princeton University
Princeton, NJ 08544

University of Chicago
Chicago, IL 60637

University of New Mexico
Albuquerque, NM 87131

University of Oregon
Eugene, OR 97403

University of Southern
California
Los Angeles, CA 90089

University of Texas, Austin
Austin, TX 78712

APPENDIX D

BOOKS OF INTEREST

Aerial Photography, Professional Techniques and Commercial Applications, by Harvey Lloyd, Amphoto, 1990.

The American Film Institute Guide to College Courses in Film & Television, Prentice Hall, 1990.

Ansel Adams: An Autobiography, by Ansel Adams with Mary Street Alinder, Amphoto, 1990.

The Art of Photography, by Bruce Barnbaum, Kendall-Hunt, 1994.

Black-and-White Darkroom Techniques, (Pub. No. KW-15), Eastman Kodak Co.

Building a Home Darkroom, (Pub. No. KW-14), Eastman Kodak Co.

The Complete Photographer, by Ron Spillman, Fisher Books, 1997.

Grundberg's Goof-Proof Photography Guide, by Andy Grunberg, Simon & Schuster, 1990.

How To Sell Your Photographs and Illustrations, by Elliott and Barbara Gordon, Allworth Press, 1990.

The Kodak Book of Practical 35mm Photography, Eastman Kodak Co.

Mastering Composition and Light, (Pub. No. LC-4), Eastman Kodak Co.

Object & Image: An Introduction to Photography, 3d. ed., by
    George M. Craven, Prentice-Hall, 1990.
Photographic Composition, by Tom Grill and Mark Scanlon,
    Amphoto, 1990.
Photography Until Now, by John Szarkowski, Little Brown, 1990.
*Photo Imaging: How to Communicate with Camera and
    Computer,* by David H. Curl, Oak Woods Media, 1997.
The Portrait, by Eastman Kodak staff, Saunders Photo, 1997.
Set Up Your Home Studio, (Pub. No. LC-13), Eastman Kodak Co.
Using Your Automatic/Autofocus Camera, (Pub. No. KW-11),
    Eastman Kodak Co.
Using Your Camera: A Basic Guide to 35mm Photography, by
    George Schaub, Amphoto, 1990.

PHOTOGRAPHY WORKSHOPS

The following list of workshops was provided courtesy of Rohn Engh of PhotoSource International in Osceola, Wisconsin.

Anderson Ranch Arts Center
  P.O. Box 5598
  Snowmass Village, CO
    81615

Arles Journees De L'Image Pro
    (JIP)
  Sylvie Havez, Press
    Relations
  1 Rue Copernic
  13200 Arles, France

Gene Boaz Workshops
  Route 5
  Benton, KY 42025

Paul Bowling Workshops
  P.O. Box 6486
  Annapolis, MD 21401-0486

Barbara Brundege Workshops
  P.O. Box 889
  Groveland, CA 95321

Laura Buckbee Workshops
  NESPA
  P.O. Box 1509
  New Milford, CT 06776

Charlene Faris Workshops
  610 West Popular #7
  Zionsville, IN 46077

China Photo Workshop Tour
  2506 Country Village
  Ann Arbor, MI 48103-6500

Colorado Mountain College
    Workshops
  Box 2208
  Breckenridge, CO 80424

Communication Unlimited
    Workshops
  P.O. Box 6405
  Santa Maria, CA 93456

Creative Vision Workshops
Orvil Stokes
317 East Winter Avenue
Danville, IL 61832

Jay Abraham Marketing
Seminars
944 Indian Peak Road,
Suite 210
Rolling Hills Estates, CA
90274

Jay Daniel Workshops
816 West Francisco
Boulevard
San Rafael, CA 94901

Art Kane Photo Workshops
1511 New York Avenue
Cape May, NJ 08204

Dillman's Sand Lake Lodge
Workshops
P.O. Box 98
Lac du Flambeau, WI 54538

Rohn Engh's Workshops
Pine Lake Farm
1910 Thirty-fifth Road
Osceola, WI 54020

Friends of Photography
Workshops
250 Fourth Street
San Francisco, CA 94103

Gerlach Nature Photography
Workshops
John Gerlach
P.O. Box 259
Chatham, MI 49816

Great American Nature
Photography Weekend
Workshop
5942 Westmere Drive
Knoxville, TN 37909-1056

Guide to Photo Tours
Bill Hammer
39 Westchester Drive
Rocky Point, NY 11778

Ron Levy Workshops
Box 3416
Soldotna, AK 99669

Los Angeles Photography
Center Workshops
412 South Park View Street
Los Angeles, CA 90057

Macro/Nature Photography
Workshops
Robert Sisson
P.O. Box 1649
Englewood, FL 34295-1649

Maine Photographic
Workshops
2 Central Street
Rockport, ME 04856

Maria Piscopo Workshops
  Creative Services Consultant
  2038 Calvert
  Costa Mesa, CA 92626

Michele Burgess Seminars
  20741 Catamaran Lane
  Huntington Beach, CA
  92646

Missouri Photo Workshop
  27 Neff Annex
  Columbia, MO 65201

Motivating the Reader and
  Selling the Graphic Arts
  Buyer Workshops
  Dynamic Graphics, Inc.
  6000 North Forrest Park
  Drive
  Peoria, IL 61614

National Press Photographers
  Association Seminars, Inc.
  3200 Croasdaile Drive,
  Suite 306A
  Durham, NC 27705

New School Workshops
  66 West Twelfth Street
  New York, NY 10011

New York Institute of
  Photography Workshops
  211 East Forty-third Street,
  Dept. WWW
  New York, NY 10017

Ogunquit Photography School
  Workshops
  Box 2234
  Ogunquit, ME 03907

Olden Workshops
  1265 Broadway
  New York, NY 10001

Owens Valley Photography
  Workshops
  P.O. Box 114
  Somis, CA 93066

Palm Beach Photographic
  Workshops
  2310 East Silver Palm Road
  Boca Raton, FL 33432

Parsons School of Design
  Workshops
  66 Fifth Avenue
  New York, NY 10011

Photo Adventures Workshops
  JoAnn Ordano,
  P.O. Box 591291
  San Francisco, CA 94118

Photographic Society of
  America Regional
  Seminars
  3000 United Founders
  Boulevard, Suite 103
  Oklahoma City, OK 73112

Photography and the Art of
Seeing Workshops
Karen Schulman
P.O. Box 771640
Steamboat Springs, CO
80477

Photography and Travel
Workshop "Directory"
Serbin Communications,
Inc.
511 Olive Street
Santa Barbara, CA 93101

Photography in Nature
Workshops
Bob Grytten
P.O. Box 3195
Holiday, FL 34690

Photo Marketing Outdoor
Workshop
Ron Sanford
P.O. Box 248
Gridley, CA 95948

Professional Workshop for the
Visual Artist
The Graphic Artists Guild
11 West Twentieth Street,
8th Floor
New York, NY 10011

Professional Workshops of
America
1090 Executive Way
Des Plaines, IL 60018

Richard Day Workshops
6382 Charleston Road
Alma, IL 62807

Rochester Institute of
Technology Workshops
P.O. Box 9887
Rochester, NY 14623-0887

David Sanger Workshops
David Sanger
920 Evelyn Avenue
Albany, CA 94706

Santa Fe Photographic
Workshops
Lisl Dennis
P.O. Box 9916
Santa Fe, NM 87504

Karen Schulman Workshops
P.O. Box 771640
Steamboat Springs, CO
80477-1640

Self-Publishing for Artists
Workshop
Harold David and Marcia
Keegan
Wilderness Studio
299 Pavonia Avenue
Jersey City, NJ 07302

Shawguides Workshops
"Directory"
Dorlene Kaplan
10 West Sixty-sixth Street,
Suite 30H
New York, NY 10023

Shenandoah Photo Workshops
P.O. Box 54
Sperryville, VA 22740

Shutterbug/PhotoPro
Workshops
5211 South Washington
Avenue
Titusville, FL 32780

Sierra Photographic
Workshops
Lewis Kemper
3251 Lassen Way
Sacramento, CA 95821

Carol Siskind Workshops
501 Course Road
Neptune, NJ 07759

63 Ranch Workshops
Sandra Cahill
Box 979-S
Livingston, MT 59047

Elaine Sorel Professional
Photographer Workshops
640 West End Avenue
New York, NY 10024

David M. Stone Photo
Workshops
7 Granston Way
Buzzards Bay, MA 02532

Carren Strock Workshops
1380 East Seventeenth Street
Brooklyn, NY 11230

Summer Photography
Workshops
Rochester Institute of
Technology
Technical & Education
Center
One Lomb Memorial Drive
Rochester, NY 14623

Texas Parks, Big Bend Ranch
Spring, Photo Workshops
Jim Carr
1019 Valley Acres Road
Houston, TX 77062

Touch of Success Photo
Seminars
Bill Thomas
P.O. Box 194
Lowell, FL 32663

Travel Photo Workshop/
Santa Fe
P.O. Box 2847
Santa Fe, NM 87504

Travel Writing Workshops
   Effin & Jules Older
   Box 163
   New St. Albany, VT 05820

Travel Writer's Workshops
   Louise Purwin Zobel
   23350 Sereno, Villa 30
   Cupertino, CA 95014

Ultimate Image Workshops
   Bob Deasy
   Box 22
   Lawton, PA 18828

Vail Valley Arts Council
      Workshops
   P.O. Box 1153
   Vail, CO 81658

Visual Studios Workshop
   31 Prince Street
   Rochester, NY 14607

Voyagers International
      Workshops
   P.O. Box 915
   Ithaca, NY 14851

Web Sites Workshops—
      Rohn Engh
   1910 Thirty-fifth Road
   Pine Lake Farm
   Osceola, WI 54020

West Coast School of
      Professional Photography
      Workshops
   Allen Roedel
   Box 395
   Imperial Beach, CA 92032

Wildlife Research Photography
      Workshops
   P.O. Box 3628
   Mammoth Lakes, CA
      93546-3628

Winona International School of
      Professional Photography
      Workshops
   1090 Executive Way
   Des Plaines, IL 60018

Woodstock Photo Workshops
   59 Tinker Street
   Woodstock, NY 12498

Norbert Wu Workshops
   1065 Sinex Avenue
   Pacific Grove, CA 93950

Truman Yeager Workshops
   921 Pine Terrace North
   Lake Worth, FL 33460-2411